COMPREHENSIVE CURRICULUM
of Basic Skills

American Education Publishing™
An imprint of Carson-Dellosa Publishing LLC
Greensboro, North Carolina

American Education Publishing™
An imprint of Carson-Dellosa Publishing LLC
P.O. Box 35665
Greensboro, NC 27425 USA

ISBN 978-1-60996-329-3

1 2 3 4 5 6 7 8 WAL 15 14 13 12 11

030117810

TABLE OF CONTENTS

INTRODUCTION

BASIC CONCEPTS AND SKILLS

READING READINESS

TABLE OF CONTENTS

MATHEMATICS READINESS

NUMBERS AND COUNTING

TIME AND MONEY

PATTERNS, GRAPHING AND THINKING SKILLS

APPENDIX

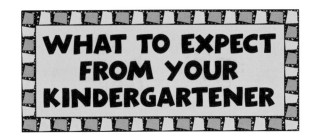

LANGUAGE

Your child . . .

- uses language effectively to express his/her needs and wants and to interact with others.
- can speak in complete sentences.
- asks many questions and looks for answers.
- enjoys being read to and talked to by adults.
- enjoys sharing information about him/herself and his/her family.
- enjoys language play, nonsense rhymes, songs, riddles and jokes.
- practices using words and language heard in school.

COGNITIVE DEVELOPMENT

Your child . . .

- has a much longer attention span and can listen to longer, more involved stories.
- can follow multiple-step directions.
- concentrates on tasks from beginning to end.
- can tell left from right.
- can name basic colors and shapes.
- can copy designs and shapes.
- can understand concepts of number, size, position and time (such as days of the week).
- associates the number of objects with the written numeral.
- can recognize letters and identify the sounds they make.
- is able to print his/her own name.
- can read familiar words.

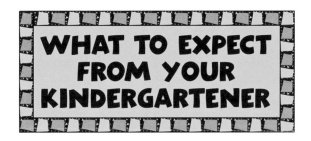

WHAT TO EXPECT FROM YOUR KINDERGARTENER

MOTOR DEVELOPMENT

Your child . . .

- can control his/her large muscles. He/she can hop on one foot; jump over objects; and throw, bounce and catch a ball easily. Your child can also run, climb, skip, tumble and dance to music.
- is able to dress and clean him/herself.
- is developing greater control over his/her small muscles. He/she should now be able to tie his/her own shoelaces and manage buttons and zippers.
- can cut on lines and use a paintbrush, crayons, markers, clay and glue.
- can print capital and lowercase letters and his/her name.

SOCIAL/EMOTIONAL DEVELOPMENT

Your child . . .

- is social and enjoys interacting with other children.
- is curious and has an active imagination.
- is confident but still needs praise and encouragement when trying new things.

DEVELOPMENTAL SKILLS CHECKLIST

This checklist is designed to help you record and assess your child's progress in the following kindergarten skills. Write the date next to each skill as your child masters it, writing any other comments you may have about your child's progress. You may also want to add to or adapt this checklist to fit your child's abilities.

BASIC SKILLS

- Names basic colors _____
- Names simple shapes _____
- Identifies opposites _____
- Understands positional concepts _____
- Names days of the week in order _____

READING READINESS

- Follows multiple-step directions _____
- Recites the alphabet _____
- Identifies capital letters in random order _____
- Identifies lowercase letters in random order _____
- Matches capital and lowercase letters _____
- Identifies sounds made by letters _____
- Identifies characters in stories _____
- Identifies setting in stories _____
- Can retell a story _____
- Identifies problem/solution in a story _____
- Reads color words _____
- Reads some words by sight _____

DEVELOPMENTAL SKILLS CHECKLIST

MATHEMATICS READINESS

- Counts objects to 20 _____
- Writes numbers to 20 _____
- Identifies numbers to 20 in random order _____
- Rote counts to 100 _____
- Counts by 10's to 100 _____
- Uses ordinal numbers _____
- Reads a graph _____
- Identifies and continues established patterns _____

WRITING READINESS

- Dictates a sentence about a picture _____
- Writes from left to right _____
- Leaves spaces between words _____
- Writes some words independently _____
- Writes own sentences using sounds _____
- Uses punctuation in sentences _____

FINE (SMALL) MOTOR SKILLS

- Colors within lines _____
- Draws shapes _____
- Holds a pencil _____
- Prints letters and numbers _____
- Cuts a line with scissors _____

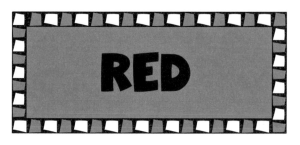

RED

Color each picture red. Then draw a picture of something else red.

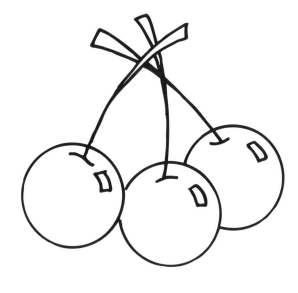

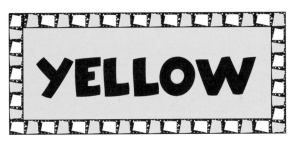

YELLOW

Name: _____

Color each picture yellow. Then draw a picture of something else yellow.

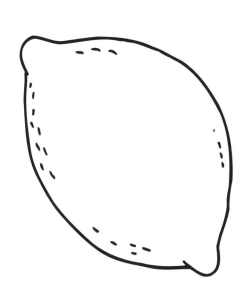

Basic Concepts and Skills

BLUE

Name: _____

Circle the blue picture in each row.

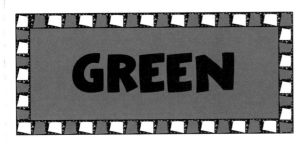

GREEN

Name: _____

Color each picture green. Then draw a picture of something else green.

Basic Concepts and Skills

ORANGE

Name:_____

Circle the orange picture in each row.

PURPLE

Name: _____

Color each picture purple. Then draw a picture of something else purple.

BLACK

Name: _____

Circle the black picture in
each row.

Name: _____

Circle the brown picture in each row.

Basic Concepts and Skills

Name: _____

Color each picture the same color as the crayon above it.

Name: _____

Color the picture.

Color the fruits and vegetables.

COLORS

Name: _____

Cut out the shapes below and glue them in the correct color box.

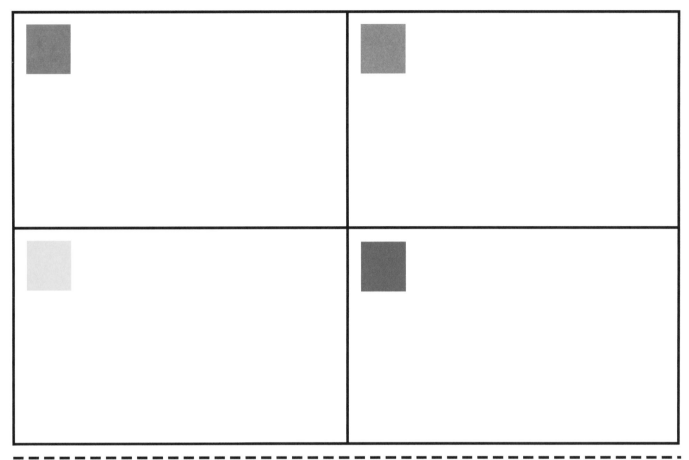

Basic Concepts and Skills

CIRCLES

Name: _____

Trace the circle below. Then draw a line under the circle in each row.

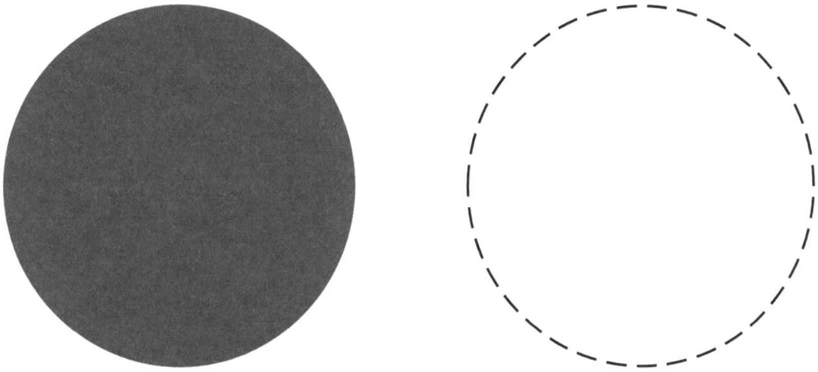

Basic Concepts and Skills

CIRCLES

Circles can be different sizes. Trace the circles below. Then color the pictures.

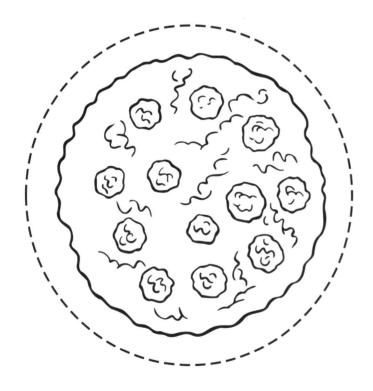

CIRCLES

Draw an **X** on the pictures that have the shape of a circle.

Basic Concepts and Skills

SQUARES

Trace the square below. Then draw a line under the square in each row.

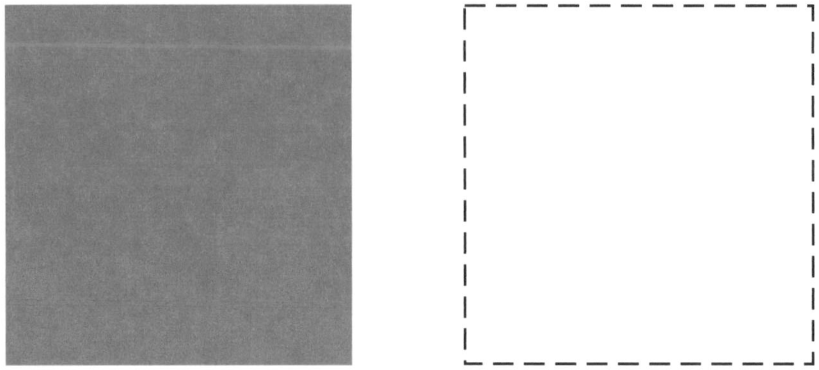

26

SQUARES

Squares have 4 sides of the same length. Help Sue get home. Color the path that has only squares.

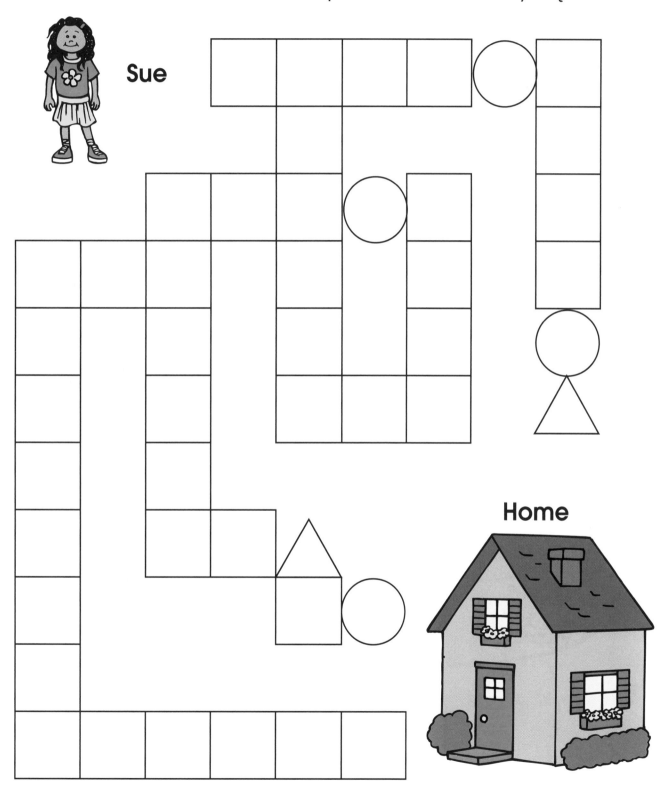

SQUARES
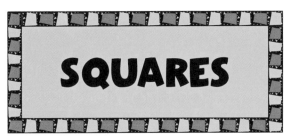

Draw an **X** on the pictures that have the shape of a square.

TRIANGLES

Trace the triangle below. Then draw a line under the triangle in each row.

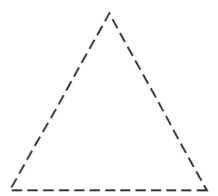

Basic Concepts and Skills

TRIANGLES

All triangles have 3 sides. Triangles can be different sizes. Trace and color the triangle shapes below.

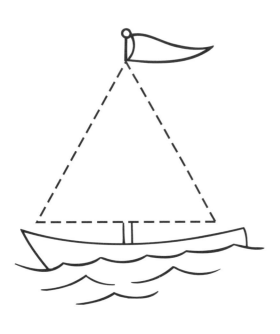

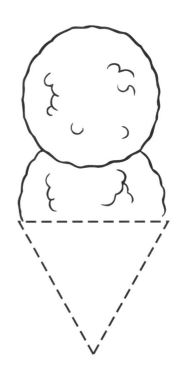

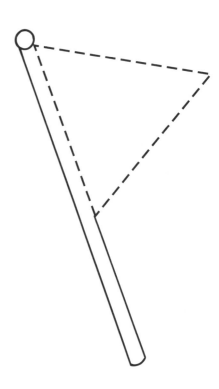

TRIANGLES

Name: _____

Draw an **X** on the pictures that have the shape of a triangle.

Basic Concepts and Skills

Name: _____

Trace and color each shape. Draw and color two more of each shape.

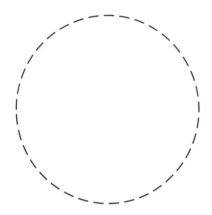

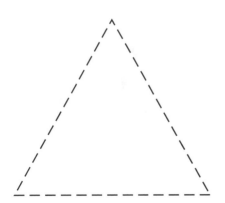

REVIEW SHAPES AND COLORS

Look at the shapes in the picture.

◆ Color the circles blue.
◆ Color the squares red.
◆ Color the triangles green.

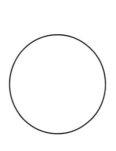
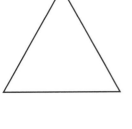
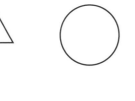

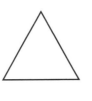
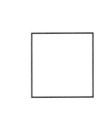
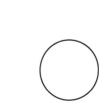
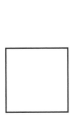

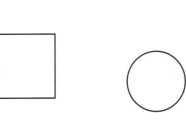

Basic Concepts and Skills

RECTANGLES

Name:_____

Trace the rectangle below. Then draw a line under the rectangle in each row.

RECTANGLES

All rectangles have 4 sides, but only the opposite sides are the same length.

Look at the shapes. Color the rectangles.

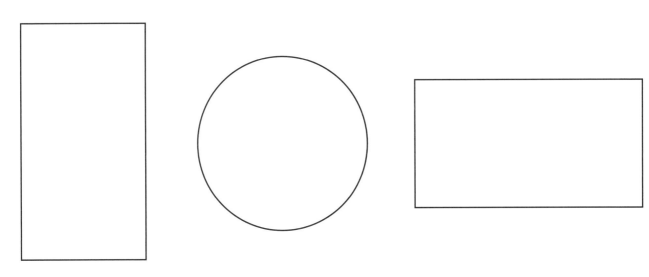

Draw a circle around each picture that has the shape of a rectangle.

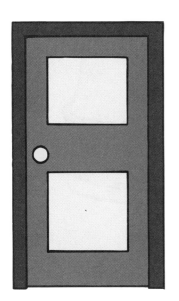

RECTANGLES

Draw an **X** on the pictures that have the shape of a rectangle.

REVIEW SHAPES

Name the shape at the beginning of each row. Circle the shape in that row that is the same.

circle   rectangle   triangle

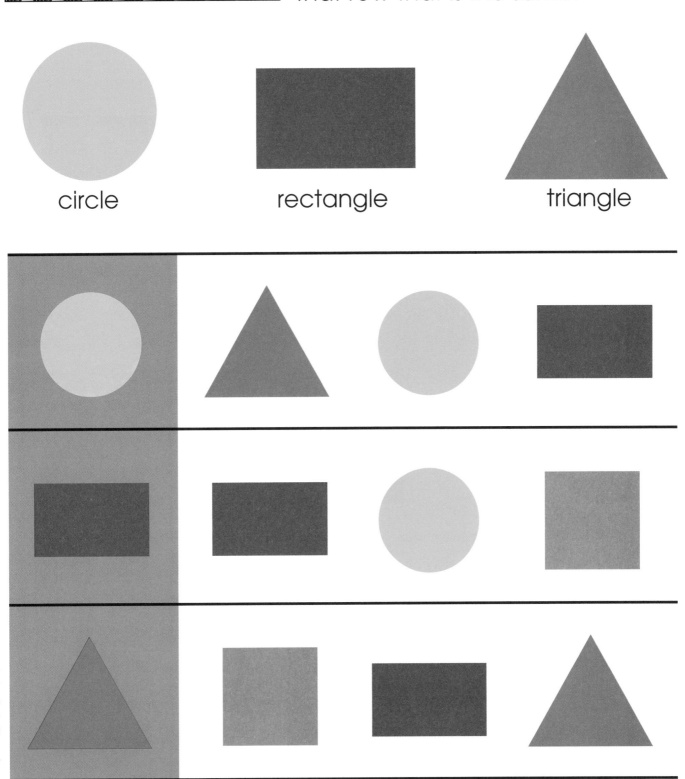

Draw a box around the circle.

Draw a box around the square.

Draw a box around the triangle.

#
REVIEW
SHAPES

Look at the picture.

◆ Color the circle.
◆ Draw a line from the rectangle to the hippo.
◆ Draw an **X** on the squares.
◆ Circle the triangle.

REVIEW
SHAPES

Color the shapes to complete this picture.

◆ Color the squares yellow.
◆ Color the triangles red.
◆ Color the rectangles green.

SHAPE ART

Name: _____

Cut out the shapes and glue them on paper to make a picture.

Basic Concepts and Skills

Name: _____

Color the circles red.

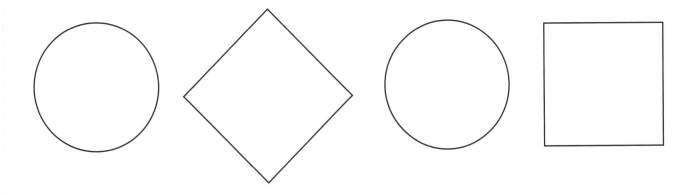

Color the rectangles green.

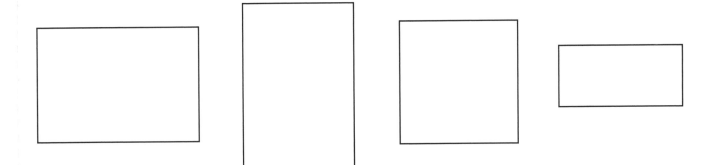

Color the triangles purple.

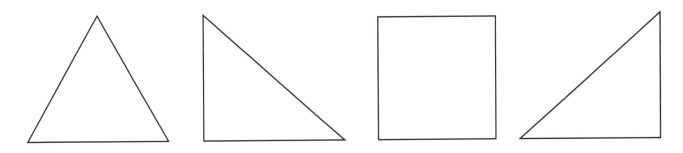

OVALS

Trace the oval below. Then draw a line under the oval in each row.

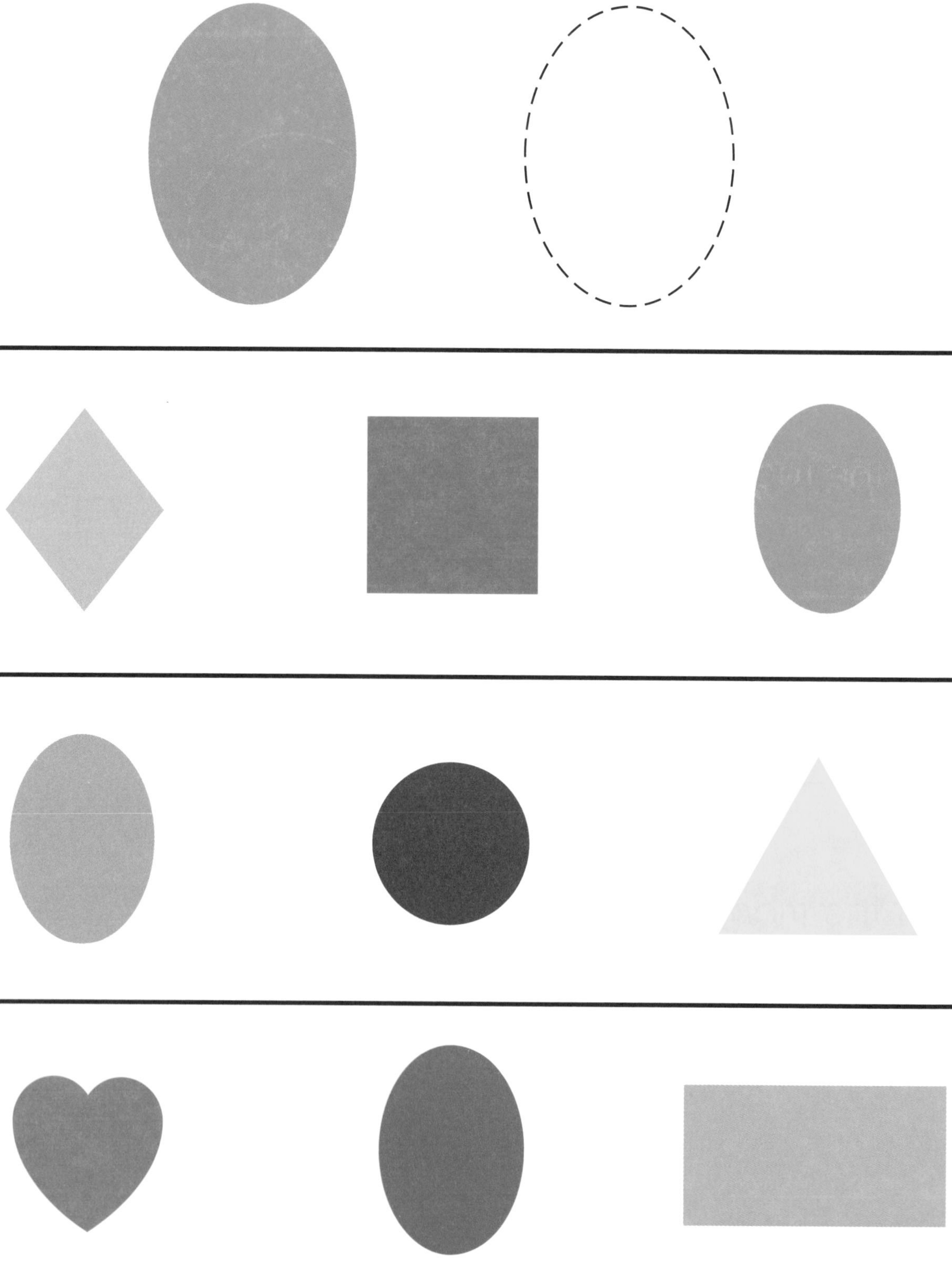

OVALS

Ovals can be different sizes.
Color the oval shapes below.

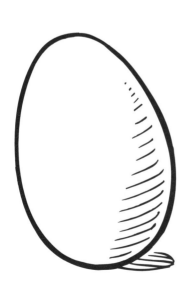

OVALS

Draw an **X** on the pictures that have the shape of an oval.

DIAMONDS

Trace the diamond below. Then draw a line under the diamond in each row.

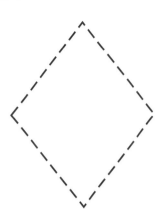

Basic Concepts and Skills

Name:_____

Trace each diamond in the designs below.

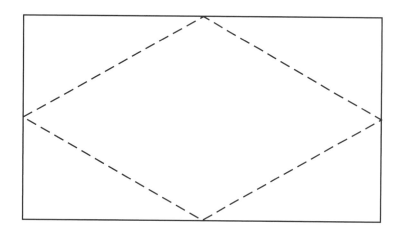

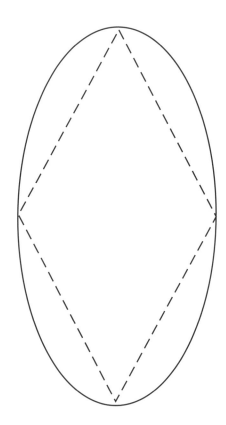

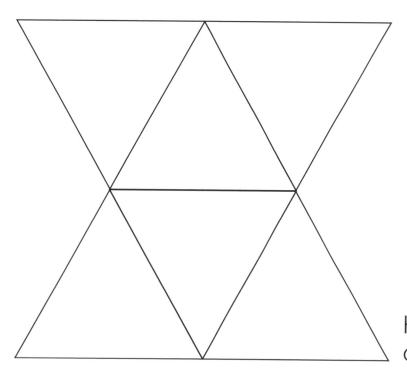

How many
did you find?_____

DIAMONDS

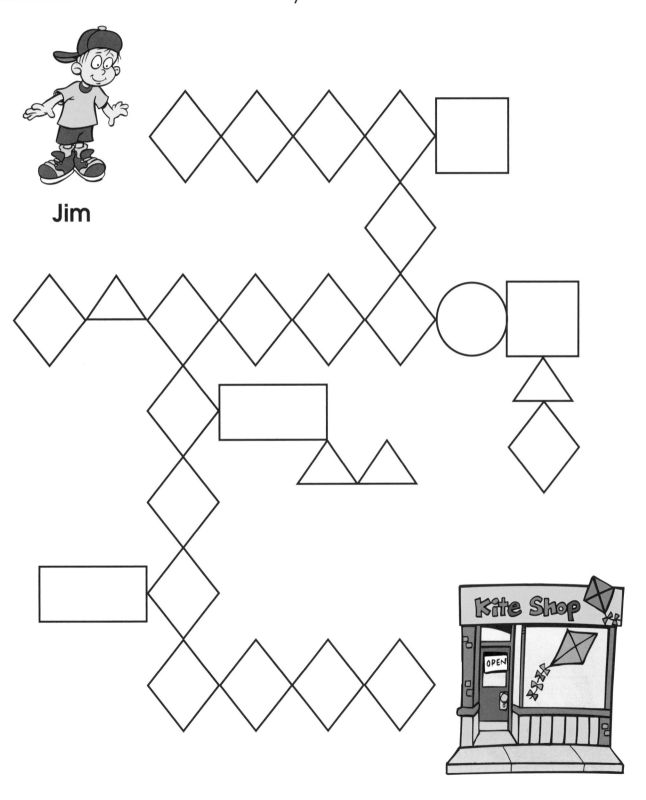

Help Jim get to the kite shop.
Color the path that has
only diamonds.

Jim

Basic Concepts and Skills

REVIEW
SHAPES

Name: _____

Draw a line to the matching pictures.

Name: _____

Trace the star below. Then draw a line under the star in each row.

Basic Concepts and Skills

STARS

Stars can be different sizes.
Color the star shapes below.

STARS

Connect the dots in order
to make your own stars.

2
•

4 •   **5**

1   **3**
•   •

2
•

4 •   **5**

1   **3**
•   •

Twinkle, twinkle, little star.
How I wonder what you are.
Up above the world so high,
Like a diamond in the sky.
Twinkle, twinkle, little star.
How I wonder what you are.

2
•

4 •   **5**

1   **3**
•   •

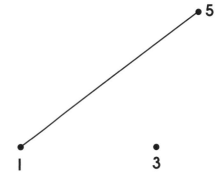

REVIEW SHAPES

Color the stars. How many stars? _____

   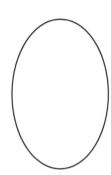

Color the ovals. How many ovals? _____

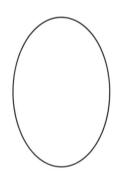  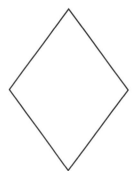 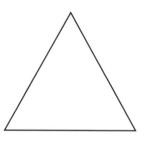

Color the diamonds. How many diamonds? _____

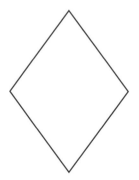 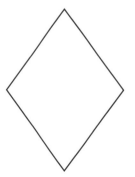 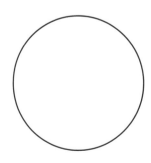 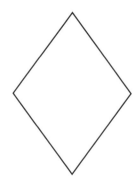

Name: _____

Look at the shapes. Answer the questions.

How many white shapes? _____

How many blue shapes? _____

How many half-white shapes? _____

How many blue stars? _____

How many white circles? _____

Name: _____

Draw a line from each shape to the basket it belongs in.

REVIEW SHAPES

Bob is looking for stars. Help him find them. Color all the stars blue.

HEARTS

Trace the heart below. Then draw a line under the heart in each row.

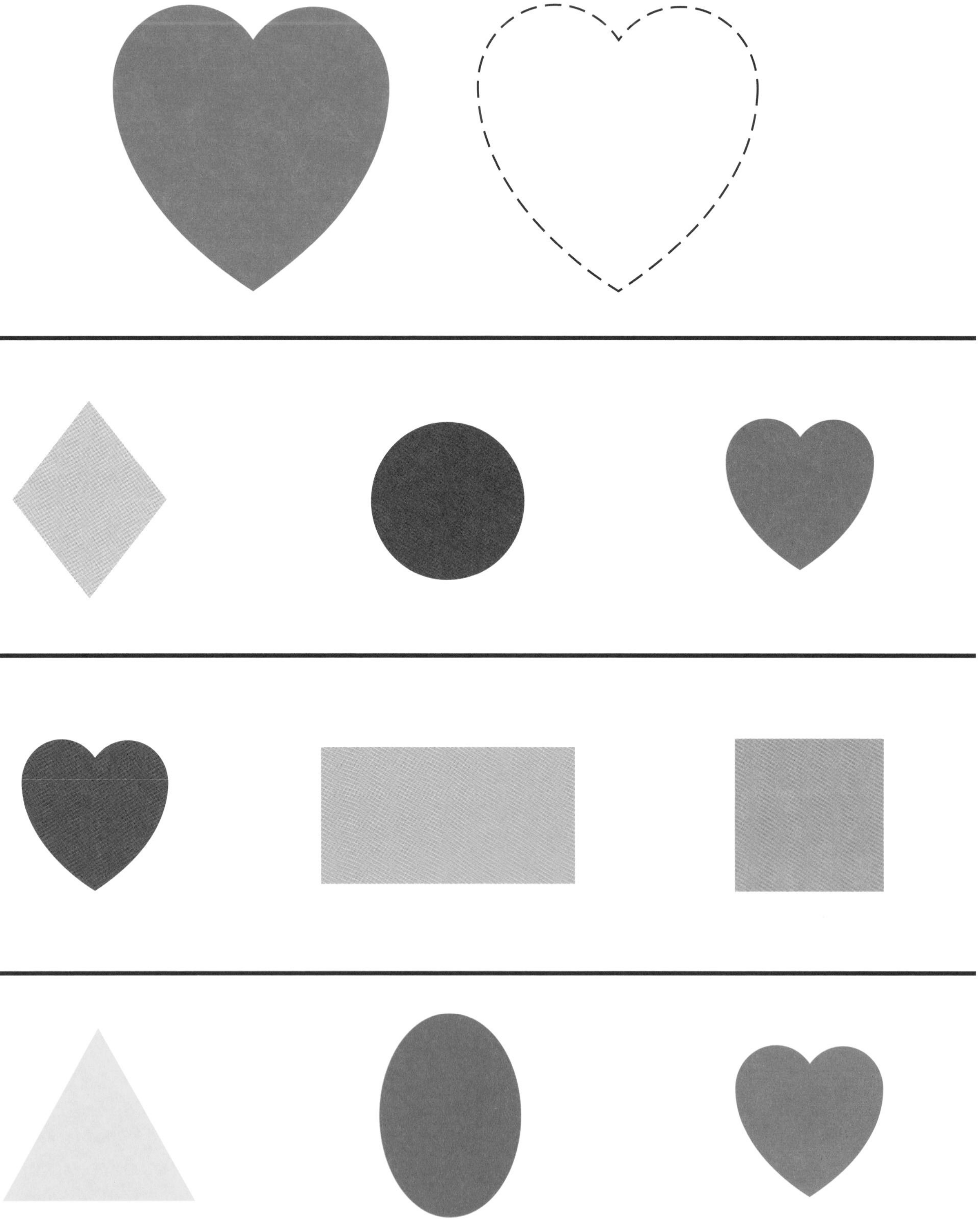

HEARTS

Name: _____

Hearts can be different sizes.
Color the heart shapes below.

HEARTS

Name:_____

Draw an **X** on the hearts in the picture below.

Color the squares purple.

 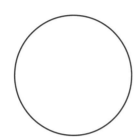 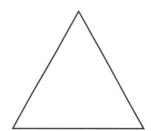 

Color the hearts blue.

 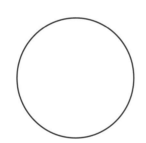  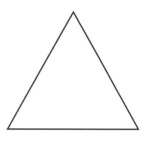

Color the diamonds yellow.

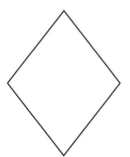  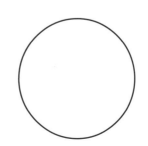 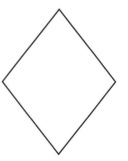

REVIEW SHAPES

Name: _____

Trace and color each shape. Draw and color two more of each shape.

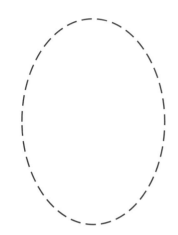

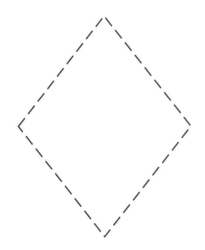

SHAPE RIDDLE

Name: _____

Read the riddle. Write and draw the answer.

I am a food.
I am cold.
I have a triangle under me.
What am I?

_____

- -

_____

Basic Concepts and Skills

SHAPE RIDDLE

Name:_____

Read the riddle. Write and draw the answer.

I can move.
You can ride in me.
I have four circles.
My seat belts keep you safe.
What am I?

DIFFERENT

Name: _____

Draw an **X** on the shapes in each row that are different from the first shape.

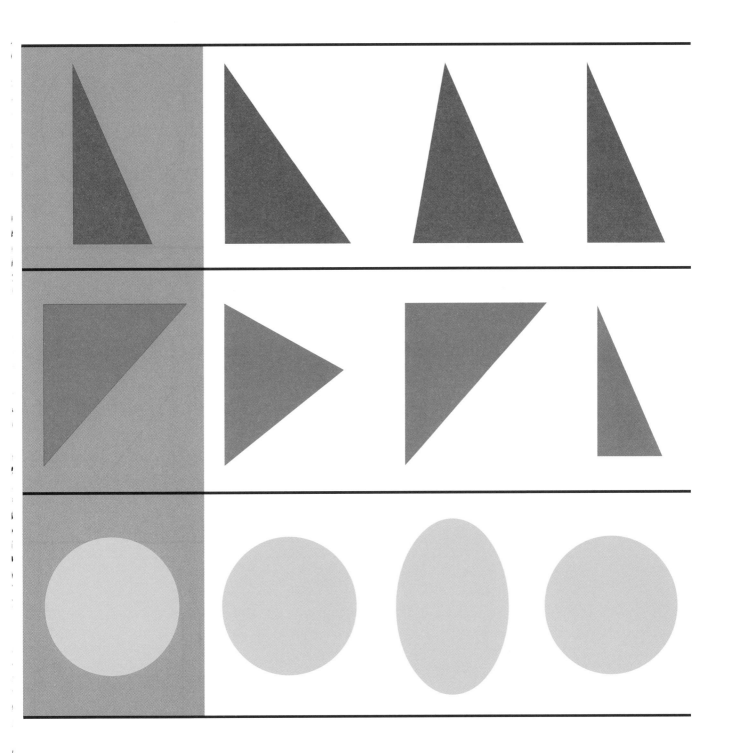

Basic Concepts and Skills

DIFFERENT

Color the shape in each row that is different.

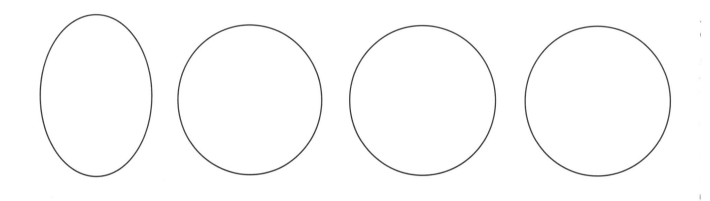

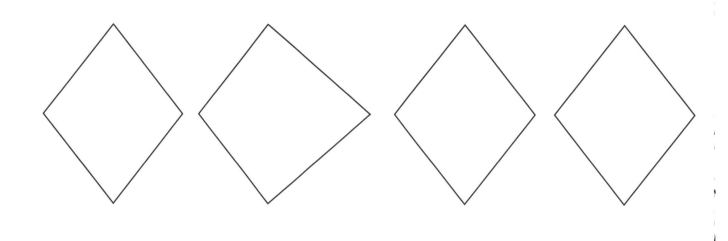

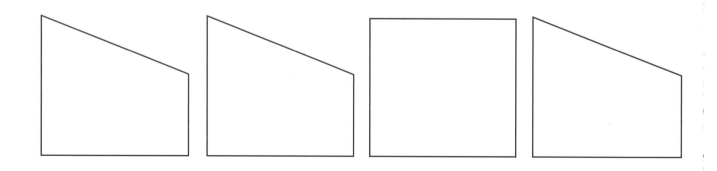

SAME

Color the shape in each row that looks the same as the first shape.

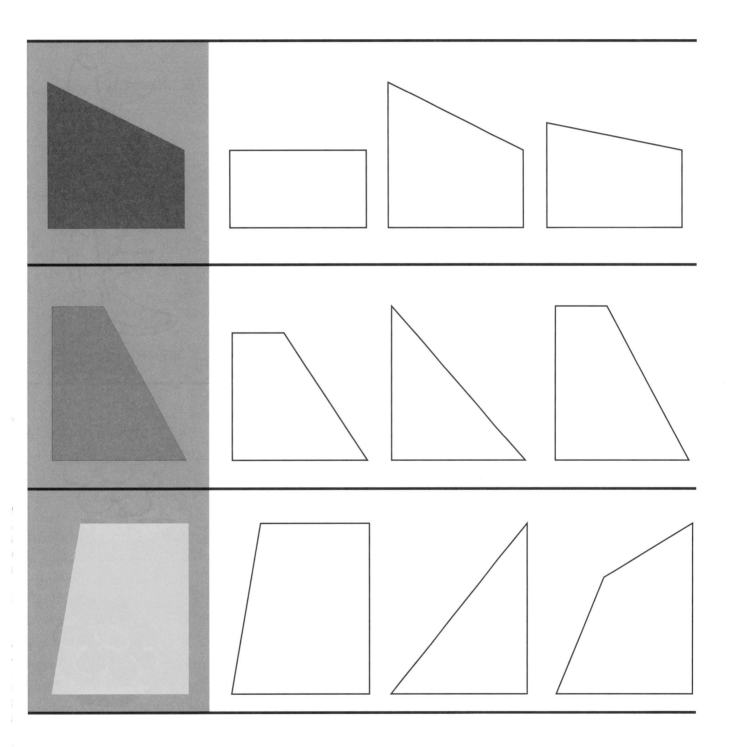

DIFFERENT

Name: _____

Draw an **X** on the picture in each box that is different.

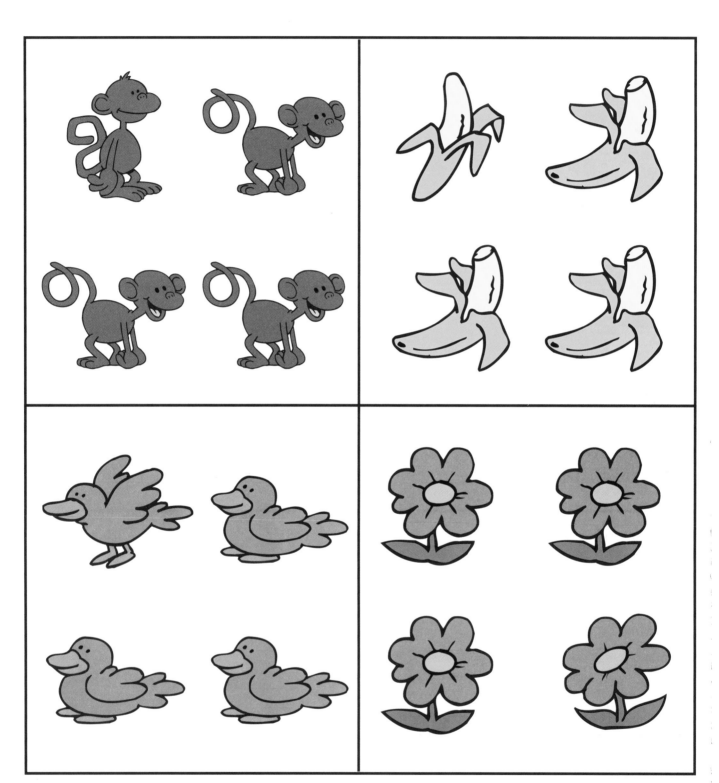

THINGS THAT GO TOGETHER

Name: _____

Color the pictures in each row that go together. Draw an **X** on the one that does not belong.

Basic Concepts and Skills

Name: _____

Color the pictures in each row that go together. Draw an **X** on the one that does not belong.

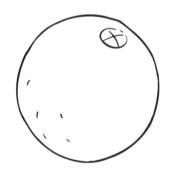   

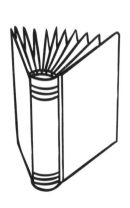   

Name: _____

Draw an **X** on the picture that does not belong. Draw another thing that does belong.

Basic Concepts and Skills

THINGS THAT GO TOGETHER

Name: _____

Draw an **X** on the picture that does not belong. Draw another thing that does belong.

THINGS THAT GO TOGETHER

Name: _____

Cut out the boxes below and on page 75. Match the pictures that go together.

Basic Concepts and Skills

THINGS THAT GO TOGETHER

Name: _____

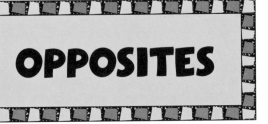

OPPOSITES

Name: _____

Opposites are things that are different in every way. Draw a line to match the opposites.

day

little

front

sad

happy

night

big

back

Basic Concepts and Skills

OPPOSITES

Draw a line to match the opposites.

old

girl

boy

full

open

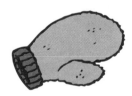

new

empty

closed

OPPOSITES

Draw a picture of the opposite.

day	night
sad	happy

Basic Concepts and Skills

OPPOSITES

Draw a picture of the opposite.

wet

dry

over

under

BIG

Name: _____

Look at the pictures in each box.
Circle the pictures that are big.

Basic Concepts and Skills

SMALL

Look at the pictures in each box.
Circle the pictures that are small.

BIG AND SMALL

Name: _____

Color the small pictures in each box orange. Color the big pictures purple.

Basic Concepts and Skills

BIG AND SMALL

Color the small pictures in each box green. Color the big pictures yellow.

Name: _____

Cut out the boxes below. Put the animals in order from smallest to biggest.

LONG

Name: _____

Circle the thing in each box that is long.

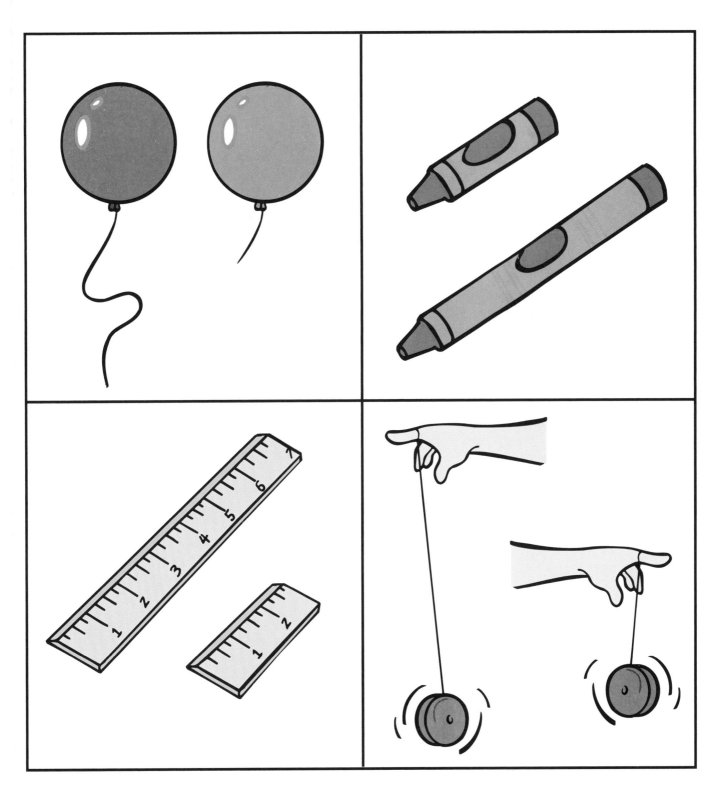

Basic Concepts and Skills

SHORT

Name: _____

Circle the thing in each box that is short.

SHORT

Circle the picture in each box that has something short.

Basic Concepts and Skills

MEASURING

Name:_____

Cut out the measuring stick at the bottom of the page. Measure each pencil below.

Example: This pencil is six boxes long.

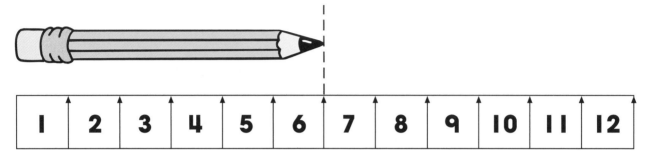

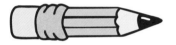 _____ boxes long

_____ boxes long

◆ Draw an **X** on the shorter pencil.
◆ Circle the longer pencil.

MEASURING

Use the measuring stick from page 90 to measure these pencils.

_____ boxes long

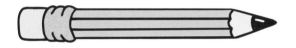

_____ boxes long

_____ boxes long

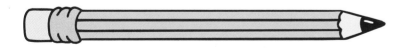

_____ boxes long

◆ Draw an **X** on the longest pencil.
◆ Circle the shortest pencil.

SHORT

Name: _____

Circle the picture in each box that is short.

TALL

Circle the picture in each box
that is tall.

Basic Concepts and Skills

Name: _____

Circle the picture that is taller. Draw an **X** on the picture that is shorter.

TALLER AND SHORTER

Name:_____

Circle the picture that is taller. Draw an **X** on the picture that is shorter.

Basic Concepts and Skills

FULL AND EMPTY

Circle the full container. Draw an **X** on the empty container.

FULL AND EMPTY

Name: _____

Circle the full container. Draw an **X** on the empty container.

ABOVE

Name: _____

Look at the picture. The sun is above the bird. Circle the pictures above the bird.

BELOW

Look at the picture. The car is below the bird. Draw an **X** on the pictures below the bird.

Basic Concepts and Skills

ABOVE AND BELOW

Circle the picture that is above the others. Draw an **X** on the picture that is below the others.

ABOVE AND BELOW

Name: _____

Color the pictures above the clouds first. Then color the pictures below the clouds.

BETWEEN

Trace and color the cat that is between the other cats.

Color the mouse that is between the other mice.

BETWEEN

Name: _____

Color each shape that is between the other shapes.

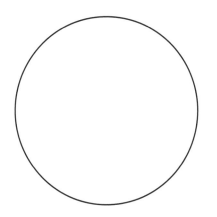 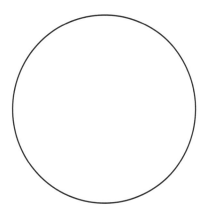 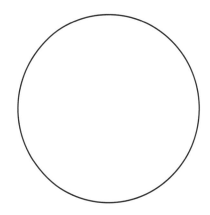

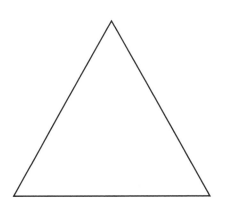 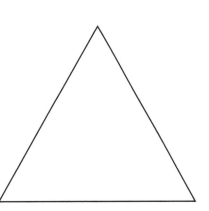 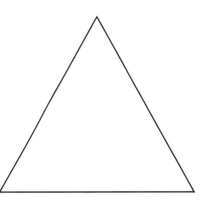

Basic Concepts and Skills

TOP TO BOTTOM

Draw a line from the top picture to the bottom picture.

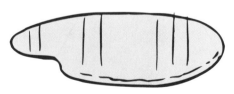

TOP TO BOTTOM

Draw a line from the top picture to the bottom picture.

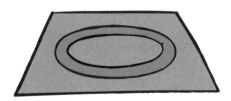  

Name: _____

Color the pictures on the left blue.
Color the pictures on the right red.

LEFT AND RIGHT

Color the pictures on the left green. Color the pictures on the right orange.

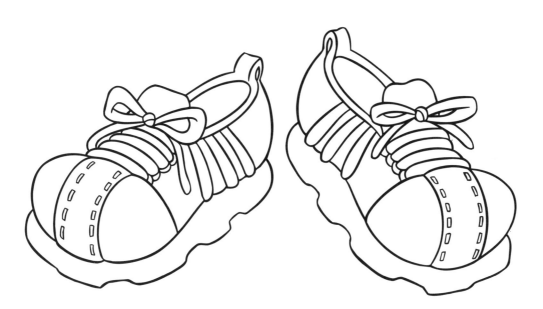

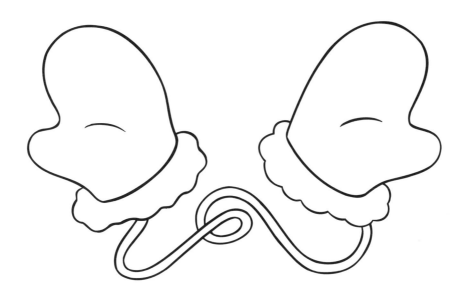

Draw a line from the picture on the left to the picture on the right.

LEFT TO RIGHT

Name: _____

Draw a line from the picture on the left to the picture on the right.

Basic Concepts and Skills

Name: _____

Names are special. We use **capital letters** to set them apart from other words.

Circle the capital letters in the names below.

Jacob   Mary

Erik   Emily

Lisa   Tom

Ann   Fred

Now, write your name. Circle the capital letter.

_____

- - - - - - - - - - - - - - - - - - -

_____

WRITING YOUR NAME

Write your name. Draw a picture of yourself doing something you like.

WRITING YOUR ADDRESS

Connect the dots in ABC order.
What did you find?

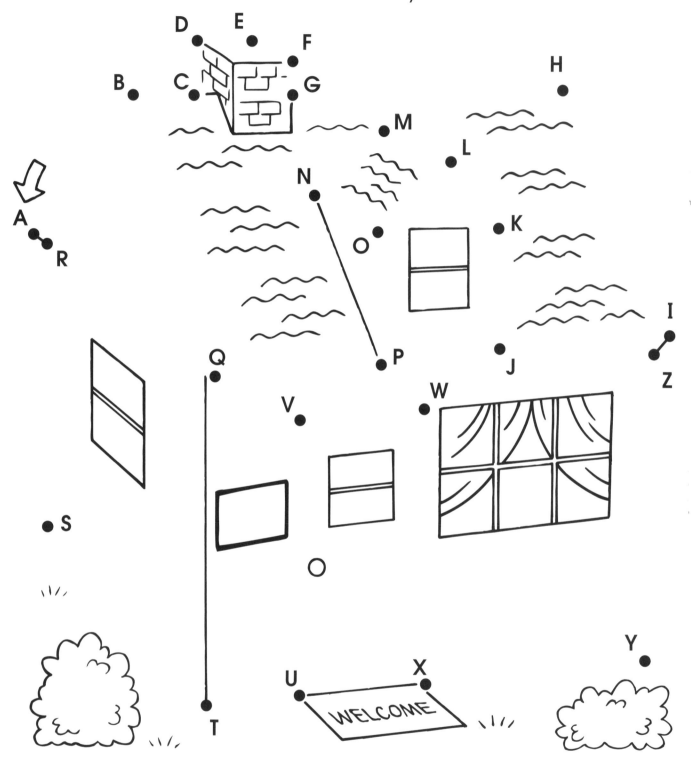

◆ Write your house or apartment number on the house.

WRITING YOUR ADDRESS

Name: _____

Write your address. Draw a picture to show where you live.

Basic Concepts and Skills

WRITING YOUR PHONE NUMBER

Name: _____

Write your phone number. Practice dialing it using the phone below.

_____

- - - - - - - - - - - - - - - - - - - -

_____

◆ Color the numbers in your phone number on the phone above.

READING READINESS

BANANA

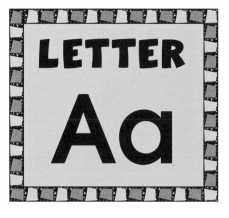

LETTER Aa

Trace and write the letter **Aa**. Start at the dot. Say the sound the letter makes as you write it.

Alphabet Express

alligator apples

Name: _____

Trace and write the letter **Bb**. Start at the dot. Say the sound the letter makes as you write it.

bear

balls

LETTER Cc

Trace and write the letter **Cc**. Start at the dot. Say the sound the letter makes as you write it.

cats

cookies

LETTER RECOGNITION
Aa, Bb, Cc

Circle the letters in each row that match the first letter.

A	N	A	V	A
a	b	a	c	a
B	B	C	B	A
b	d	a	b	a
C	O	C	D	C
c	a	c	c	o

Name: _____

Look at the letter each insect is holding. Circle the same letter below.

V   X   A

R   B   F

O   Q   C

o   a   c

g   b   k

f   a   c

Name: _____

Trace and write the letter **Dd**. Start at the dot. Say the sound the letter makes as you write it.

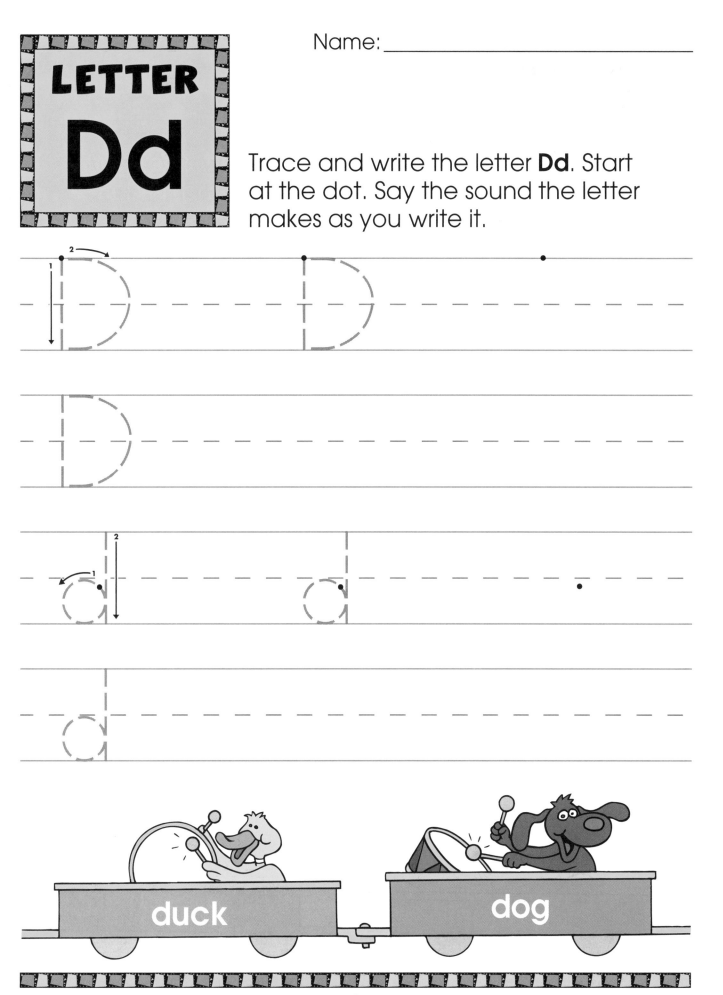

duck

dog

LETTER
Ee

Trace and write the letter **Ee**. Start at the dot. Say the sound the letter makes as you write it.

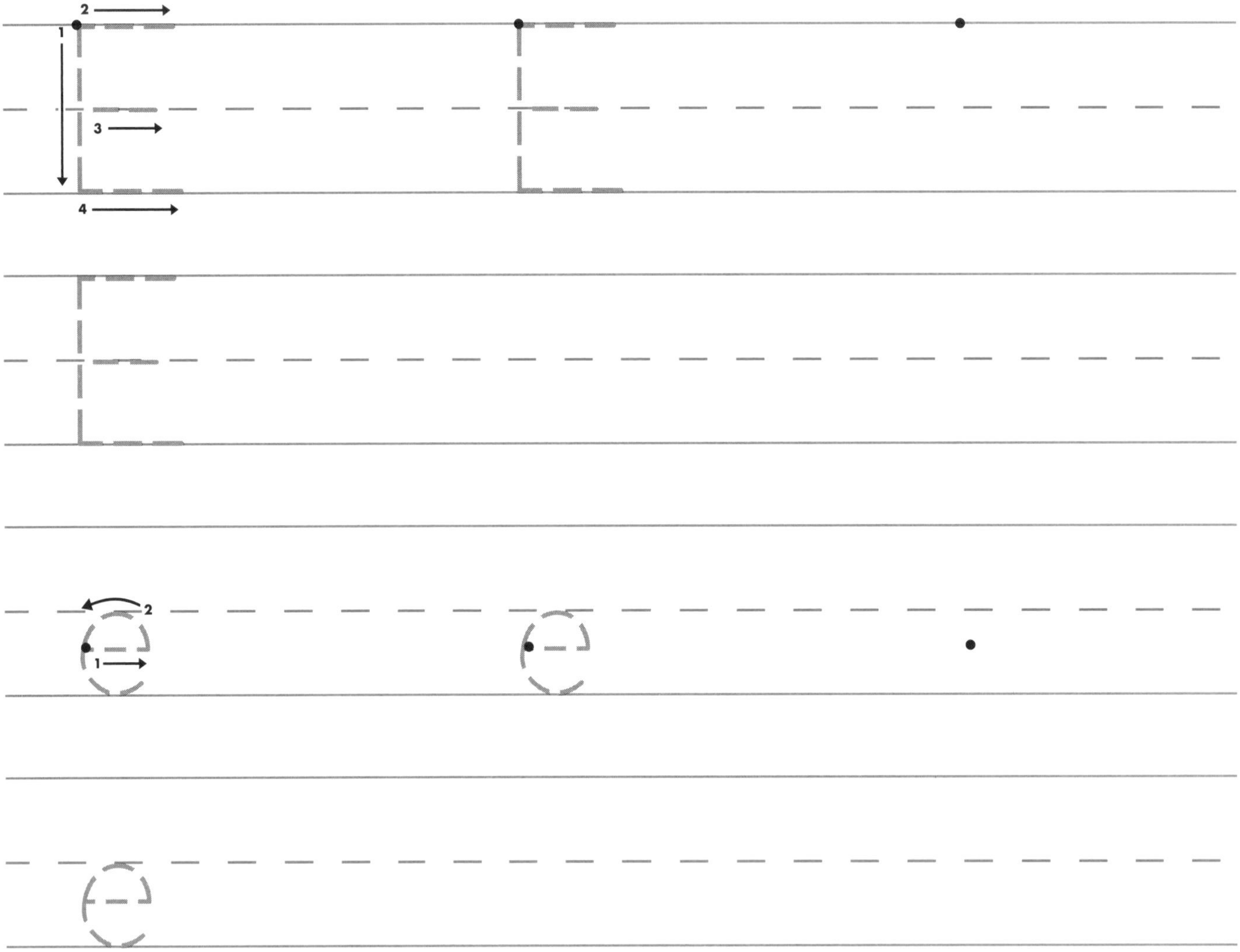

elephant

eggs

Name: _____

Trace and write the letter **Ff**. Start at the dot. Say the sound the letter makes as you write it.

frog

fish

Name: _____

Circle the letters in each row that match the first letter.

D	B	G	D	B
d	b	d	a	d
E	H	F	E	E
e	e	a	b	e
F	E	F	E	A
f	t	f	l	o

Name: _____

Look at the uppercase letter in each row. Color each picture with a matching lowercase letter.

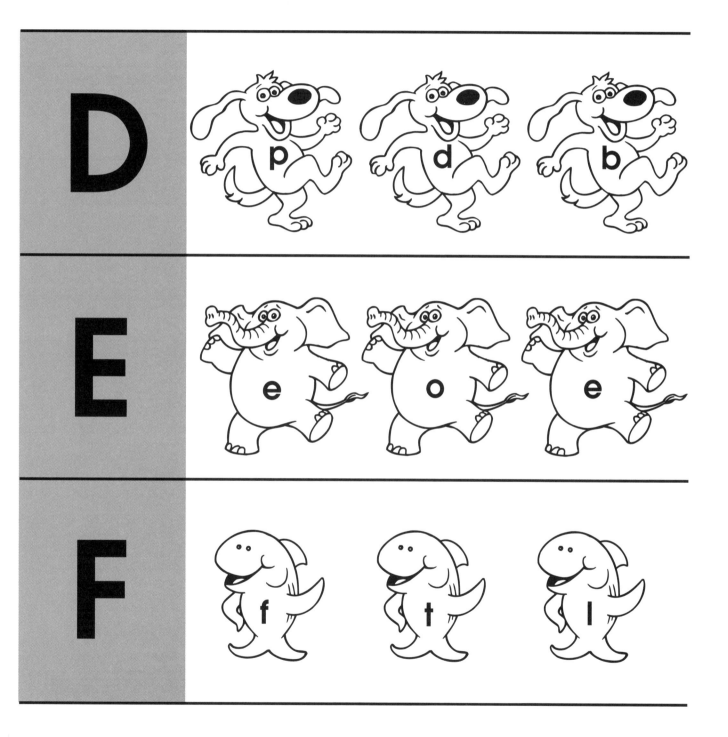

D

E

F

LETTER Gg

Trace and write the letter **Gg**. Start at the dot. Say the sound the letter makes as you write it.

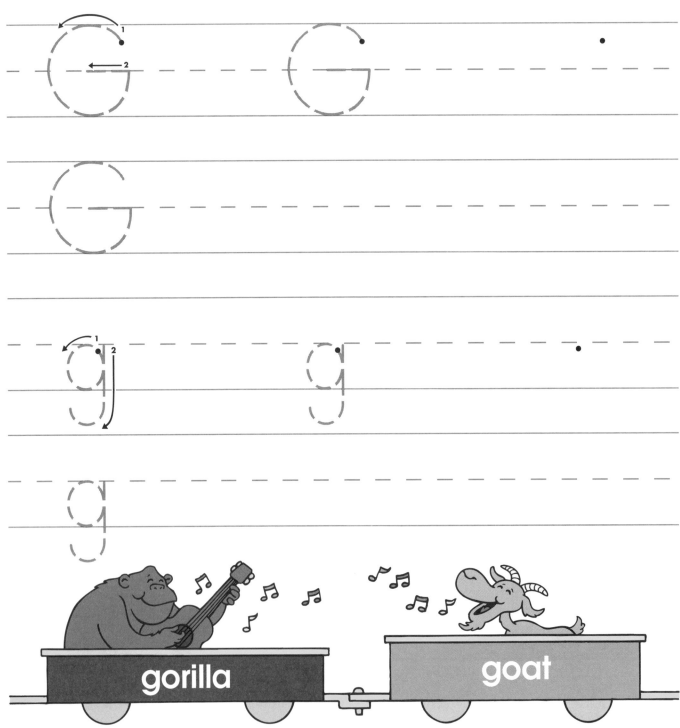

gorilla

goat

Name: _____

Trace and write the letter **Hh**. Start at the dot. Say the sound the letter makes as you write it.

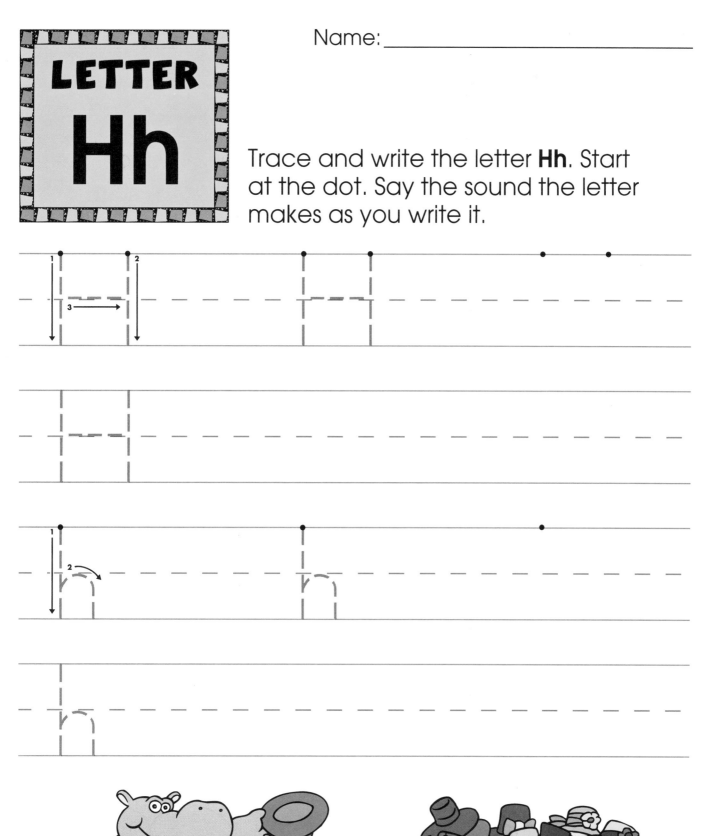

hippo

hats

LETTER
I i

Trace and write the letter **Ii**. Start at the dot. Say the sound the letter makes as you write it.

iguana

ice cream

Name: _____

Circle the letters in each row that match the first letter.

G	C	G	O	B
g	g	p	q	g
H	E	F	H	I
h	d	n	b	h
I	H	I	L	A
i	t	i	l	i

Reading Readiness

Name: _____

Draw a line from each uppercase letter to its matching lowercase letter.

Gg Hh Ii

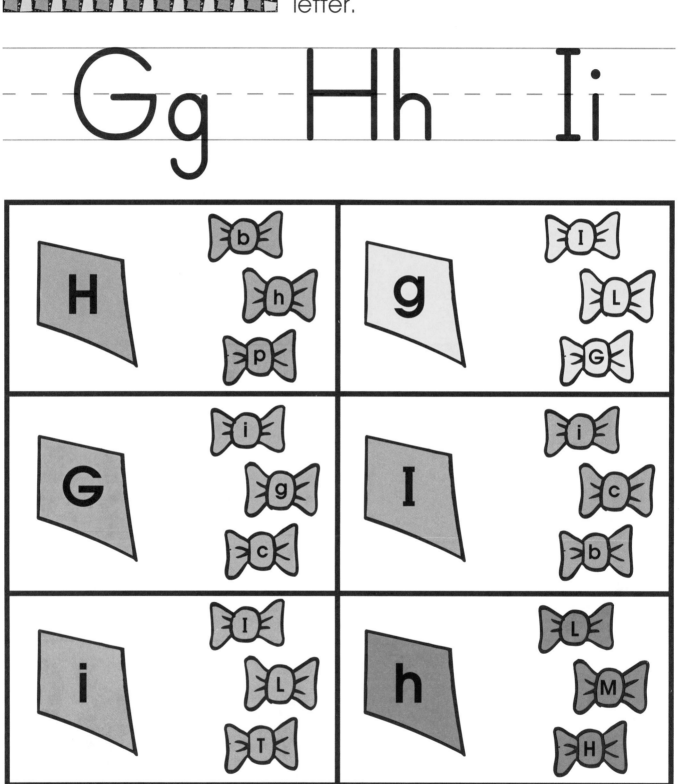

LETTER Jj

Trace and write the letter **Jj**. Start at the dot. Say the sound the letter makes as you write it.

jaguar

jam

131

Name: _____

Help the walrus get back to the sea by following the letters in ABC order.

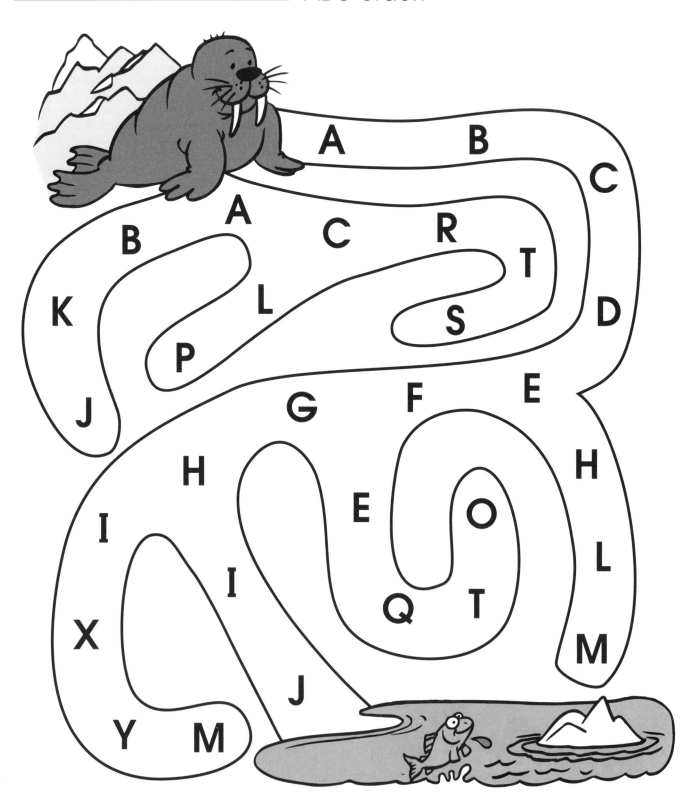

Name: _____

Find out what the elves are making. Draw a line to connect the dots in ABC order.

Name: _____

Trace and write the letter **Kk**. Start at the dot. Say the sound the letter makes as you write it.

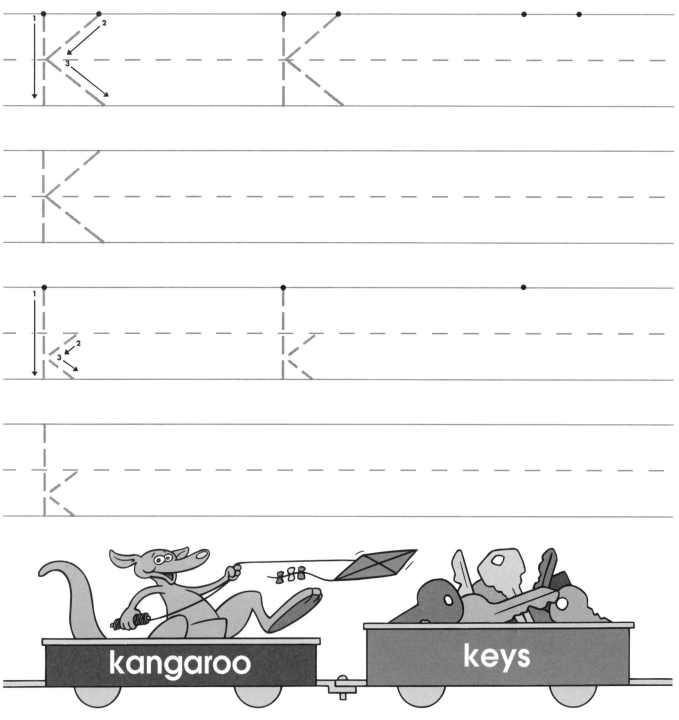

kangaroo

keys

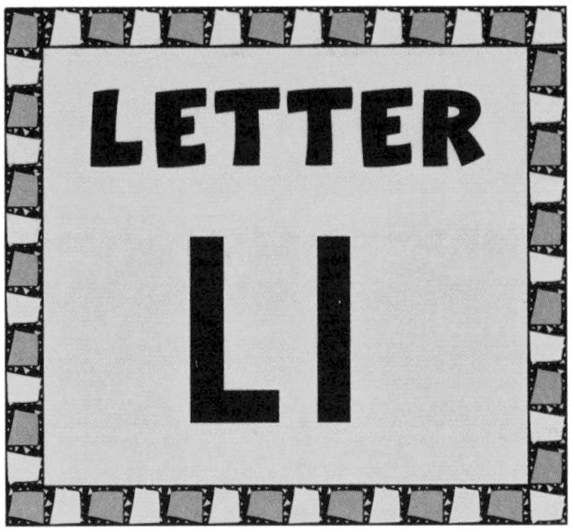

LETTER
Ll

Trace and write the letter **Ll**. Start at the dot. Say the sound the letter makes as you write it.

lion

lollipops

Name: _____

Circle the letters in each row that match the first letter.

J	J	U	L	J
j	g	j	q	i
K	N	F	H	K
k	l	h	k	b
L	J	I	L	U
l	t	i	l	i

Name: _____

Draw a line from each uppercase letter to its matching lowercase letter. Then color the pictures.

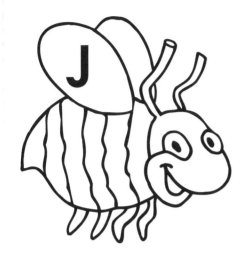

LETTER Mm

Name: _____

Trace and write the letter **Mm**. Start at the dot. Say the sound the letter makes as you write it.

monkey

money

REVIEW
Aa-Mm

Help Adam get to the playground.
Follow the letters in ABC order.

Name: _____

Trace and write the letter **Nn**. Start at the dot. Say the sound the letter makes as you write it.

newt

nest

LETTER

Oo

Trace and write the letter **Oo**. Start at the dot. Say the sound the letter makes as you write it.

ostrich

octopus

Name: _____

Circle the letters in each row that match the first letter.

M	H	M	n	L
m	M	a	m	n
N	M	N	m	N
n	n	m	a	n
O	O	D	B	O
o	a	O	c	o

Name: _____

Color each fish that has an uppercase and lowercase letter that match.

 Oo

 Mm

 Oc

 Nm

 Nn

 Oo

 Nz

 Mm

 Mm

 Nn

 Oa

 Nn

Reading Readiness

LETTER Pp

Name: ______________________

Trace and write the letter **Pp**. Start at the dot. Say the sound the letter makes as you write it.

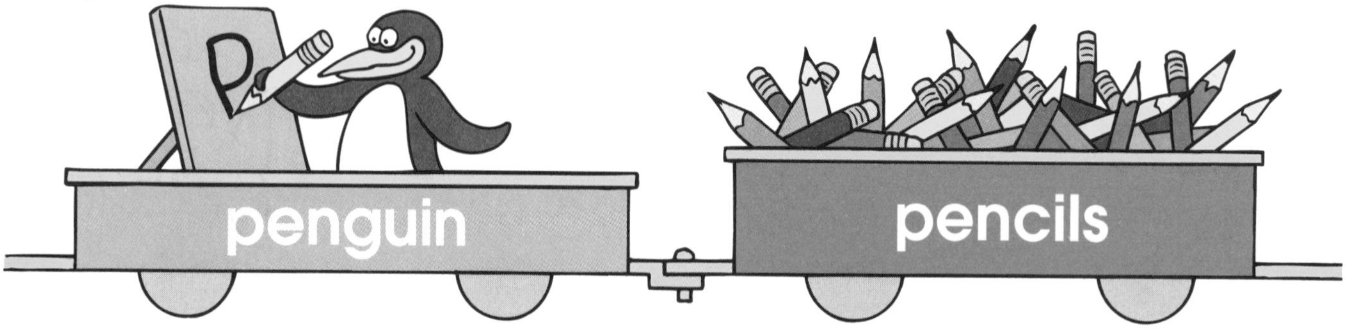

P
penguin
pencils

LETTER Qq

Trace and write the letter **Qq**. Start at the dot. Say the sound the letter makes as you write it.

quarters

queen

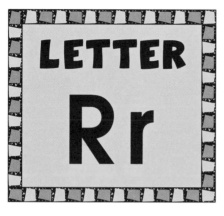

LETTER Rr

Name: _____

Trace and write the letter **Rr**. Start at the dot. Say the sound the letter makes as you write it.

rabbit

rocks

LETTER RECOGNITION

Pp, Qq, Rr

Name: ____________________

Circle the letters in each row that match the first letter.

P	D	P	O	b
p	p	d	q	b
Q	O	Q	G	Q
q	p	q	d	b
R	R	B	P	R
r	r	n	m	r

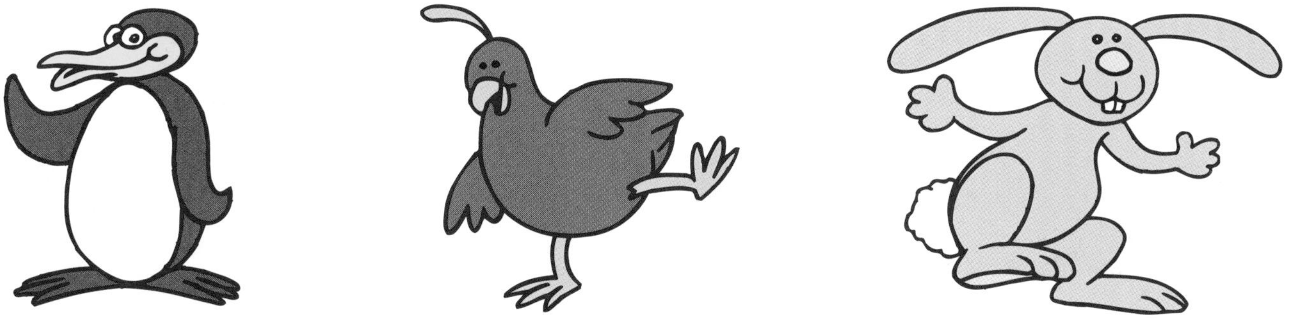

LETTER Ss

Trace and write the letter **Ss**. Start at the dot. Say the sound the letter makes as you write it.

seal

sea horse

LETTER
Tt

Trace and write the letter **Tt**. Start at the dot. Say the sound the letter makes as you write it.

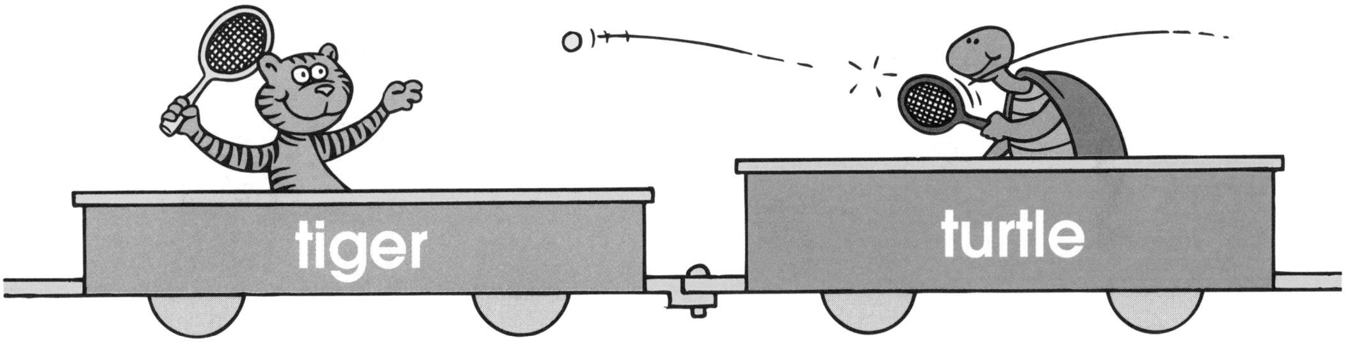

tiger

turtle

Name:_____

Draw a line from each uppercase letter to its matching lowercase letter.

LETTER
Uu

Name: _____

Trace and write the letter **Uu**. Start at the dot. Say the sound the letter makes as you write it.

unicorn

umbrellas

Name: _____

Circle the letters in each row that match the first letter.

S	P	S	B	S
s	o	a	s	e
T	I	P	L	T
t	f	I	t	i
U	U	D	U	O
u	u	n	m	n

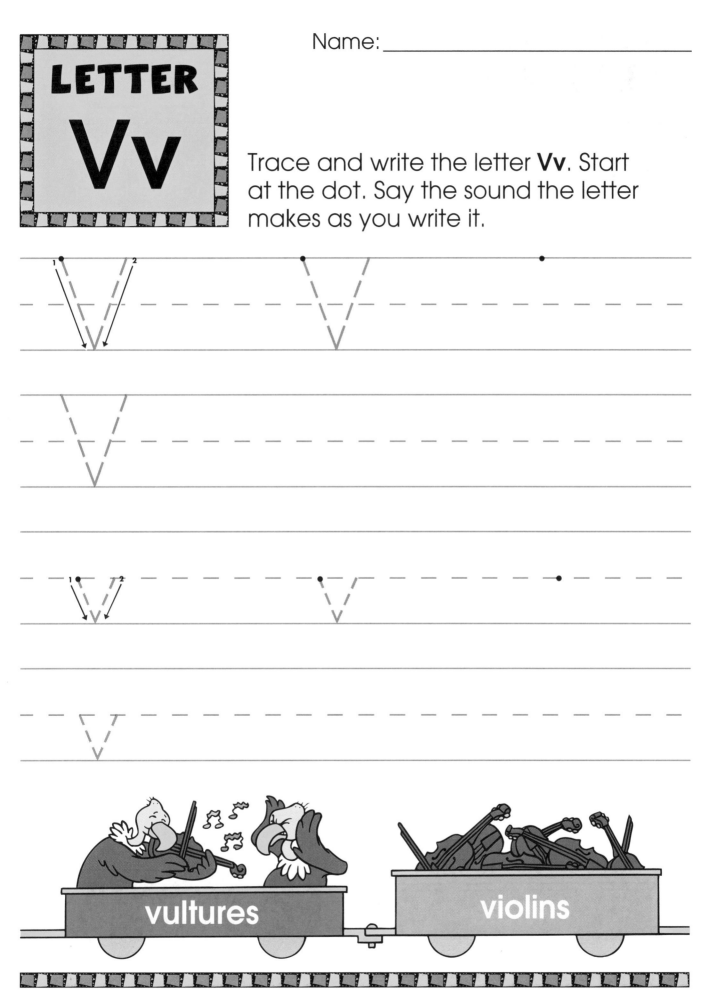

LETTER Vv

Name: _____

Trace and write the letter **Vv**. Start at the dot. Say the sound the letter makes as you write it.

vultures

violins

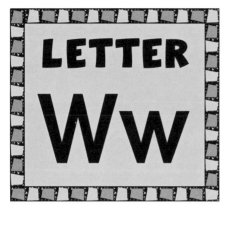

LETTER Ww

Trace and write the letter **Ww**. Start at the dot. Say the sound the letter makes as you write it.

whale

walrus

LETTER

Xx

Trace and write the letter **Xx**. Start
at the dot. Say the sound the letter
makes as you write it.

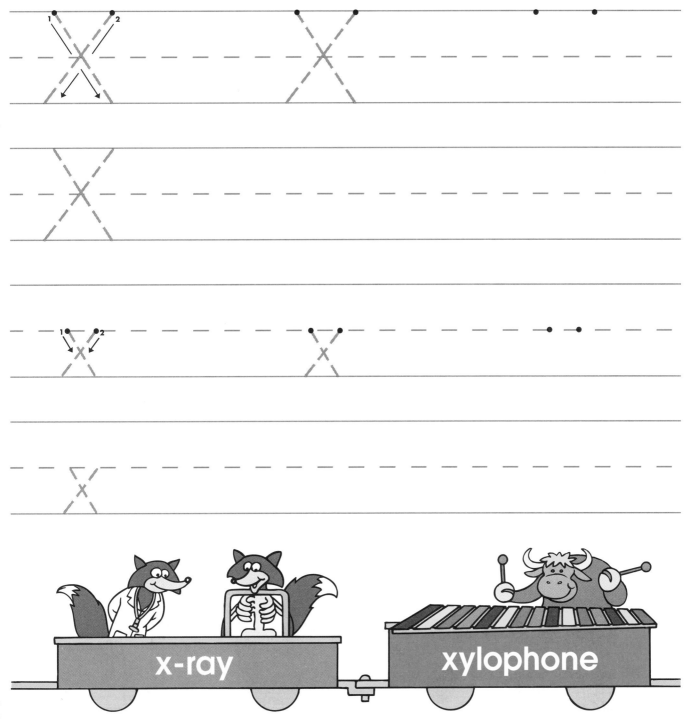

x-ray

xylophone

Name: _____

Circle the letters in each row that match the first letter.

V	W	V	A	N
V	W	X	v	y
W	V	M	A	W
w	w	v	x	m
X	Y	X	V	K
x	y	k	x	z

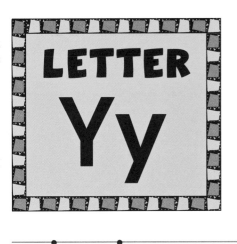

LETTER Yy

Trace and write the letter **Yy**. Start at the dot. Say the sound the letter makes as you write it.

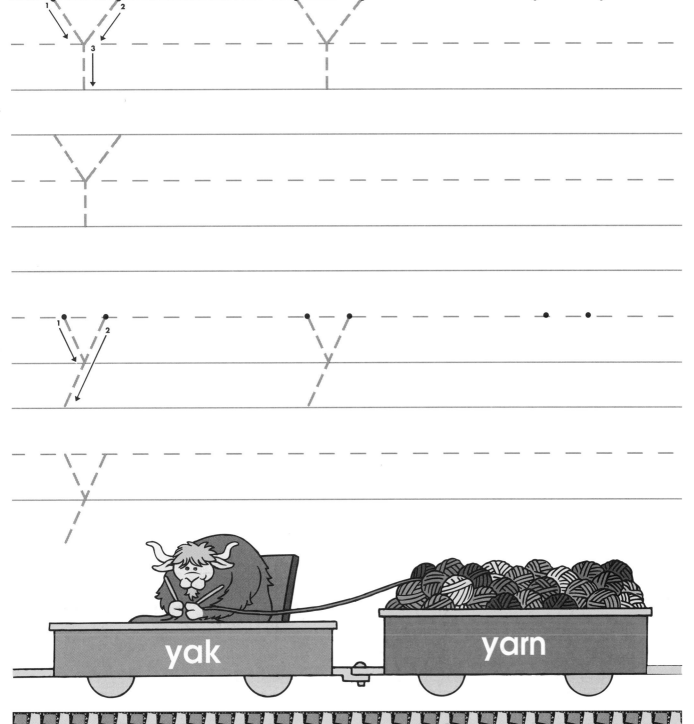

yak

yarn

LETTER Zz

Name: ______________________

Trace and write the letter **Zz**. Start at the dot. Say the sound the letter makes as you write it.

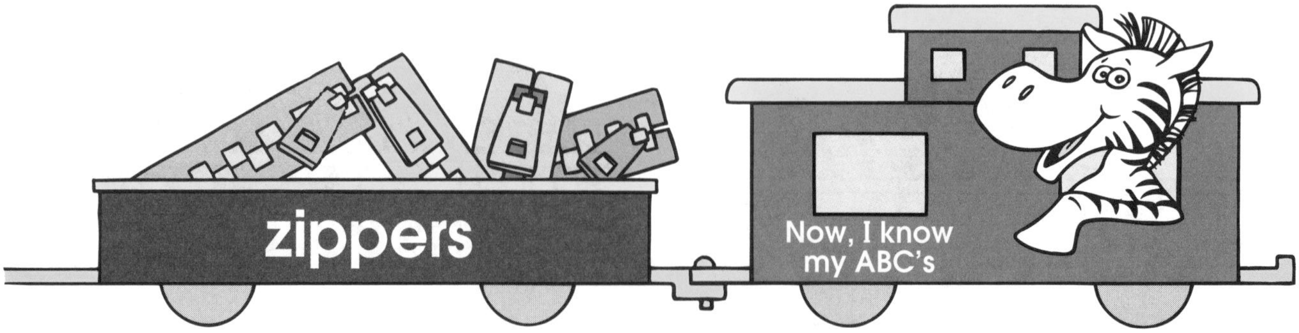
zippers
Now, I know my ABC's

Name: _____

Circle the letters in each row that match the first letter.

Y	W	Y	V	X
y	w	x	v	y
Z	N	M	Z	W
z	n	z	x	m

REVIEW
Uu–Zz

Write the missing uppercase or lowercase letter for each tie.

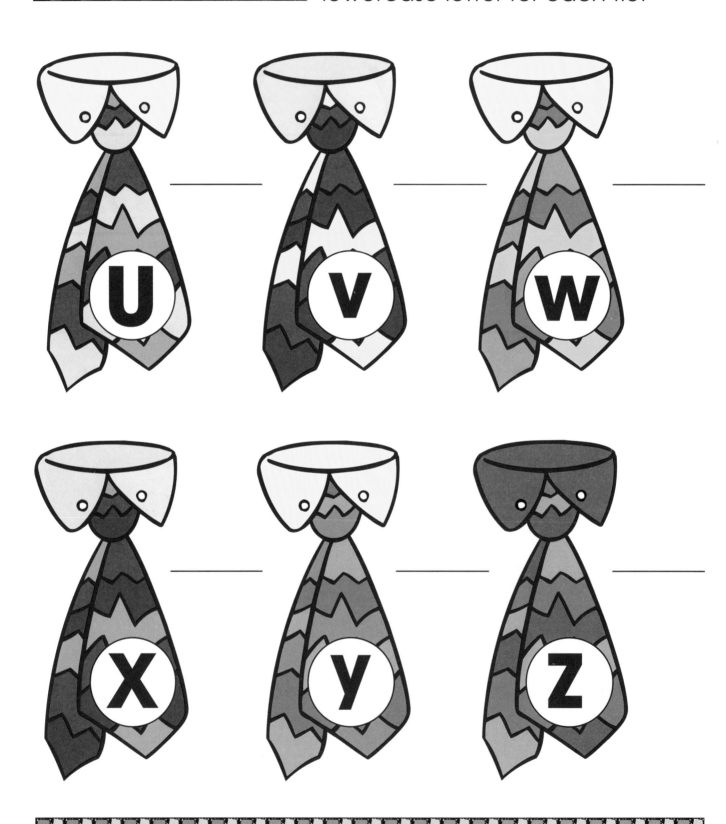

ABC ORDER

Connect the dots in ABC order.
Color the picture.

Reading Readiness

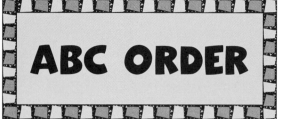

ABC ORDER

Name: _____

Connect the dots in ABC order.
Color the picture.

ABC ORDER

Name: _____

Connect the dots in ABC order.
Color the picture.

Name: _____

Write the missing uppercase letters to complete the alphabet.

Name: _____

Write the missing lowercase
letters to complete the alphabet.

Name: _____

Circle each hidden letter of the alphabet below.

Name: _____

Color all the letters red. Color all the numbers blue. Write the letter message below.

2	Y	O	U	7	4	1	0	5
7	6	10	A	R	E	9	3	8
4	1	S	P	E	C	I	A	L

_____ _____ _____   _____ _____

_____ _____ _____ _____ _____ _____ _____ !

Reading Readiness

SHORT VOWEL Aa

These pictures begin with the letter **Aa**.
Color these pictures.

astronaut

apple

ant

animals

SHORT VOWEL

Aa

Short Aa is the sound at the beginning of the word **alligator**. Color the pictures that begin with the **short Aa** sound.

SHORT VOWEL Aa

Short Aa is the sound at the beginning of the word **animals**. Say each picture name. Circle the pictures whose names have the **short Aa** sound.

SHORT VOWEL Aa

Name each picture. Write the correct letter at the beginning of each word. The first one is done for you.

h   m

hat

c   d

 at

b   p

at

f   r

at

SHORT VOWEL
Aa

Read the words. Draw a line from each word to the picture that matches it.

bat   **hat**   **cat**

SHORT VOWEL Aa

Name: _____

Say each picture name. Write **a** to complete each word below.

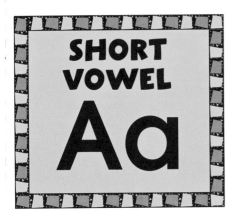

m   p   c   t

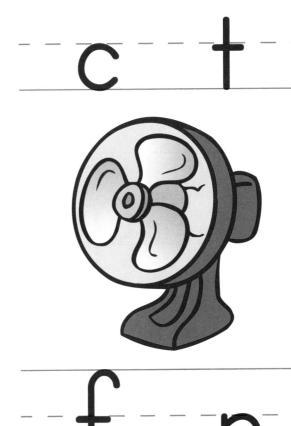

c   n   f   n

Reading Readiness

Name: _____

Write the letter **a** to complete each word below. Draw a line to match the word with its picture.

p _ n

m _ n

b _ g

v _ n

SHORT VOWEL Aa

Cut out the hat and feather. Cut on the dotted lines to make slits. Slip the feather through the hat. Slide the feather and read each new word.

◆ Diagram

Reading Readiness

BEGINNING CONSONANT
Bb

Name: _____

These pictures begin with the letter **Bb**.
Color these pictures.

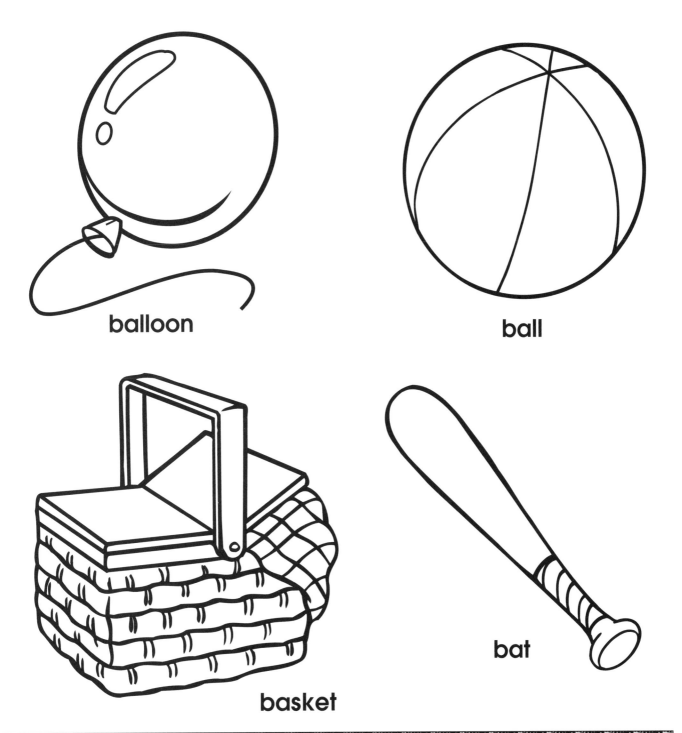

balloon

ball

basket

bat

BEGINNING CONSONANT
Bb

Say each picture name. If the picture name begins with the same sound as **ball**, color the space.

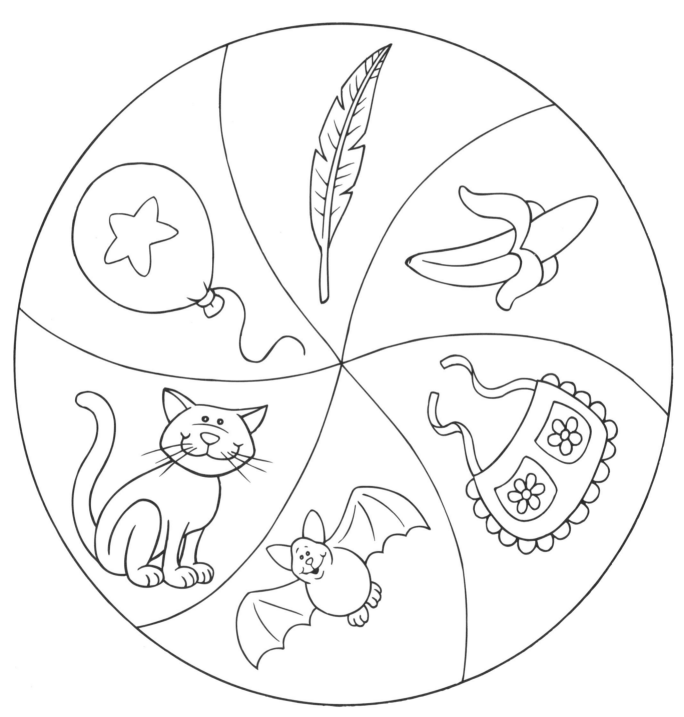

BEGINNING CONSONANT Cc

Name: _____

These pictures begin with the letter **Cc**.
Color these pictures.

cat

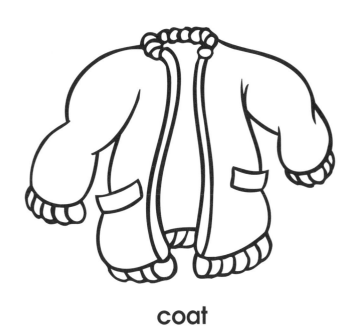

coat

cookie

car

Reading Readiness

BEGINNING CONSONANT Cc

Name: _____

Cut out the pictures at the bottom. If the picture begins with the same sound as **caterpillar**, glue it on the caterpillar to give him some spots.

BEGINNING SOUNDS
Aa, Bb, Cc

Name: _____

Say the sound the letters make. Circle the pictures in each row that begin with the letter shown.

Aa			
Aa			
Bb			
Bb			
Cc			
Cc			

Reading Readiness

Name: _____

These pictures begin with the letter **Dd**.
Color these pictures.

dog

doughnut

duck

doll

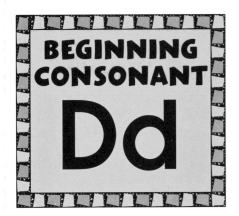

BEGINNING CONSONANT Dd

Say the picture names in each box on the door. Circle the picture whose name begins with the same sound as **dinosaur**.

Name: _____

Look at each picture. Write the letter for the beginning sound under each picture.

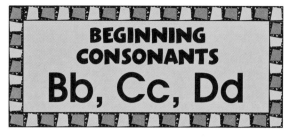

_____

_ _ _ _

_____

_____

_ _ _ _

_____

_____

_ _ _ _

_____

_____

_ _ _ _

_____

_____

_ _ _ _

_____

_____

_ _ _ _

_____

Name: _____

These pictures begin with the letter **Ee**.
Color these pictures.

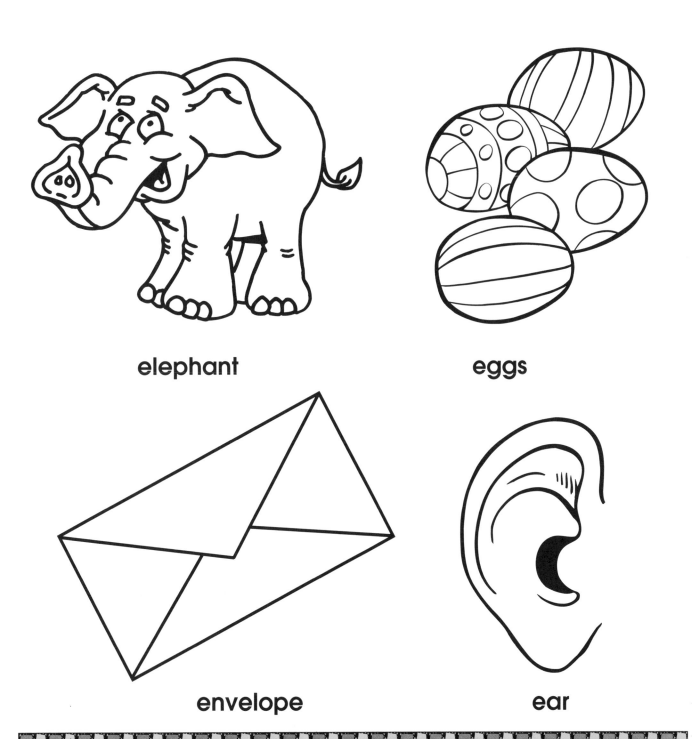

elephant

eggs

envelope

ear

SHORT VOWEL Ee

Name: _____

Short Ee is the sound at the beginning of the word **eggs**. Color the pictures that begin with the **short Ee** sound.

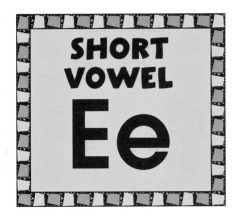

SHORT VOWEL Ee

Name: _____

Short Ee is the sound in the middle of the word **hen**. Help the hen get to the barn. Follow the path with the pictures whose names have the **short Ee** sound.

SHORT VOWEL Ee

Say the name of each picture. Write the letter **e** to complete each word below.

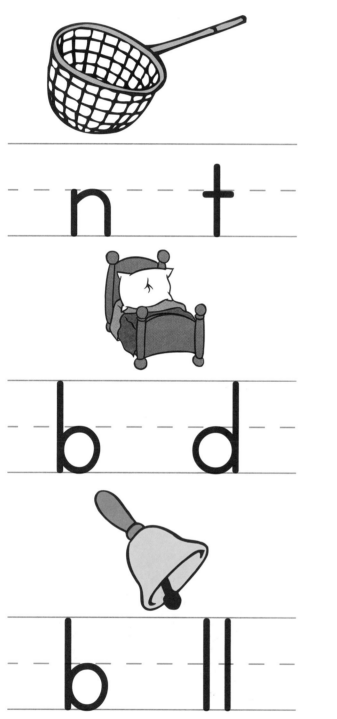

n ___ t   p ___ n

b ___ d   j ___ t

b ___ ll   h ___ n

SHORT VOWEL
Ee

Say the name of each picture. Write the letter **e** to complete each word below.

10

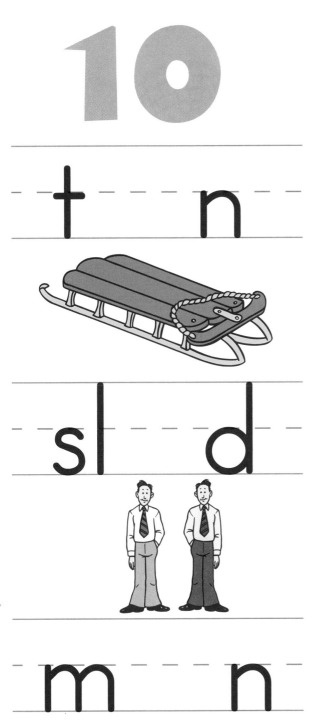

t ___ n

s ___ d

m ___ n

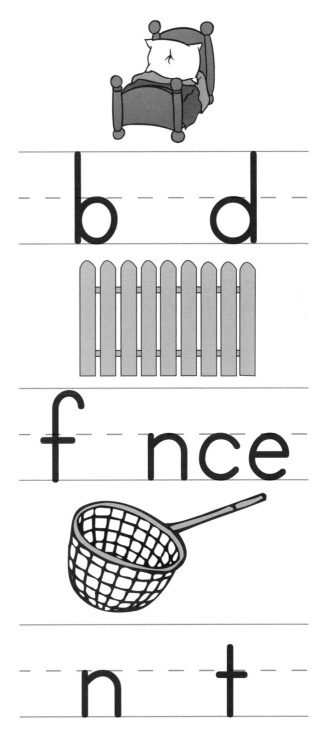

b ___ d

f ___ nce

n ___ t

Read the words. Circle the picture that matches the word.

| net |
| fence |
| bell |
| ten |

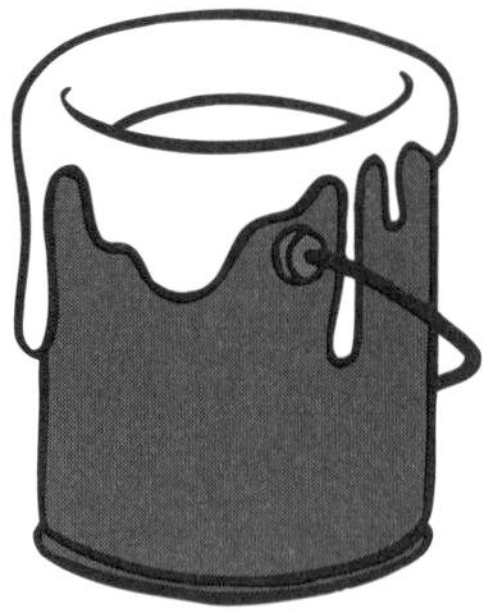

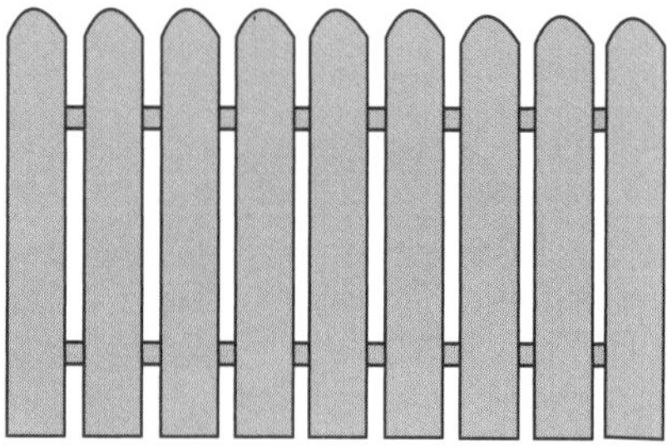

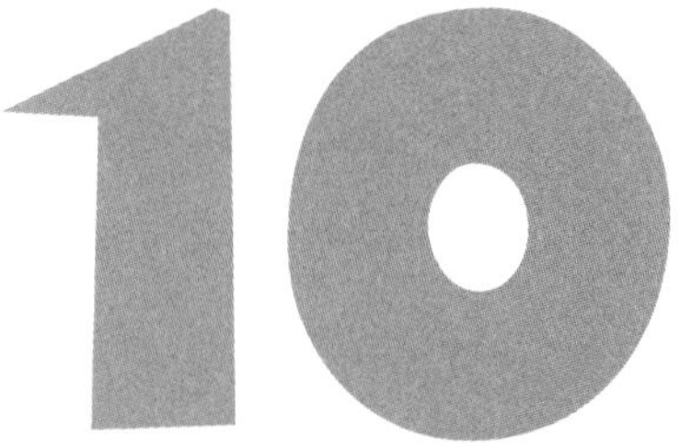

Make a flip book to read words. Cut out the cards below. Put the big card with the word **ten** on the bottom. Put the letter cards on top of the big card.

t en

d h m p

◆ Staple the cards on the far left side.
◆ Then flip the cards and read each word.

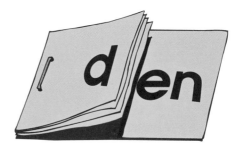

Reading Readiness

BEGINNING CONSONANT Ff

These pictures begin with the letter **Ff**.
Color these pictures.

feather

frog

fish

fire

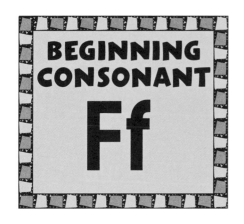
Name: _____

Look at the bubbles below. Say each picture name. If the picture begins with the same sound as **fish**, color it blue.

BEGINNING CONSONANT
Ff

Say each picture name. If the picture name begins with the same sound as **flower**, color the picture.

Dd, Ee, Ff

Name: _____

Say the sound the letters make. Circle the pictures in each row that begin with the letter shown.

Dd			
Dd			
Ee			
Ee			
Ff			
Ff			

BEGINNING CONSONANT
Gg

Name: _____

These pictures begin with the letter **Gg**.
Color these pictures.

goose

girl

goat

gate

Reading Readiness

BEGINNING CONSONANT
Gg

Say each picture name. Circle the pictures whose names begin with the same sound as **goggles**.

BEGINNING CONSONANT

Hh

These pictures begin with the letter **Hh**.
Color these pictures.

house

hat

horse

heart

BEGINNING CONSONANT
Hh

Say each picture name. If the picture begins with the **Hh** sound, color the **hat**.

Name: _____

Say the sound the letters make. Circle the pictures in each row that begin with the letter shown.

| **Ff** |  |

| **Gg** |  |

| **Hh** |    |

Reading Readiness

SHORT VOWEL I i

Name: _____

These pictures begin with the letter **I i**.
Color these pictures.

ink

inch

igloo

insect

SHORT VOWEL
I i

Short Ii is the sound at the beginning of the word **igloo**. Color the pictures that begin with the **short Ii** sound.

SHORT VOWEL I i

Name: _____

Short Ii is the sound in the middle of the word **dish**. Say the name of each picture. Draw lines from the dish to the pictures with the **short Ii** sound.

Name: _____

Read the words. Draw a line from each word to the picture that matches it.

six

pig

fish

SHORT VOWEL I i

Short **Ii** is the sound you hear in the middle of the word **pig**. Say each picture name. Write **i** to complete each word below.

ch __ ck

g __ ft

p __ n

w __ g

f __ n

b __ b

SHORT VOWEL
I i

Say each picture name. Circle the word that names the picture. Write it on the line.

fin _____

- - - - - - - - - - - - - -

tin _____

pin _____

- - - - - - - - - - - - - -

bin _____

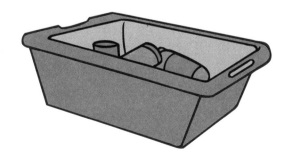

bin _____

- - - - - - - - - - - - - -

fin _____

SHORT VOWEL
I i

Read each word below. Then write the word on the line.

six

_____

- - - - - - - - - - - - - -

_____

wig

_____

- - - - - - - - - - - - - -

_____

pig

_____

- - - - - - - - - - - - - -

_____

SHORT VOWEL
I i

Cut out the bin and paper. Cut on the dotted lines to make slits. Slip the paper through the slits on the bin. Slide the paper and read each new word.

in

◆ Diagram

Name: _____

Say the sound the letters make.
Circle the pictures in each row
that begin with the letter shown.

Gg			
Gg			
Hh			
Hh			
Ii			
Ii			

BEGINNING CONSONANT Jj

These pictures begin with the letter **Jj**.
Color these pictures.

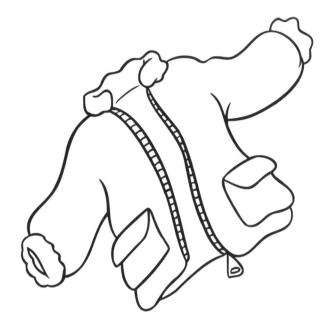

jacket

jar

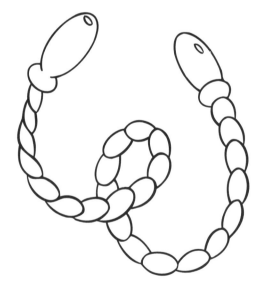

jump rope

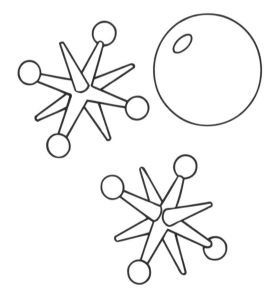

jacks

BEGINNING CONSONANT Jj

What is Jamie wearing today? Say each picture name. Color the spaces with the **Jj** sound blue. Color the other spaces yellow.

◆ What is Jamie wearing? _____

Name: _____

These pictures begin with the letter **Kk**.
Color these pictures.

kite

king

kitten

key

BEGINNING CONSONANT Kk

Look at the pictures on the kite's tail. Say each picture name. If the picture begins with the same sound as **kite**, color it orange. Then color the kite.

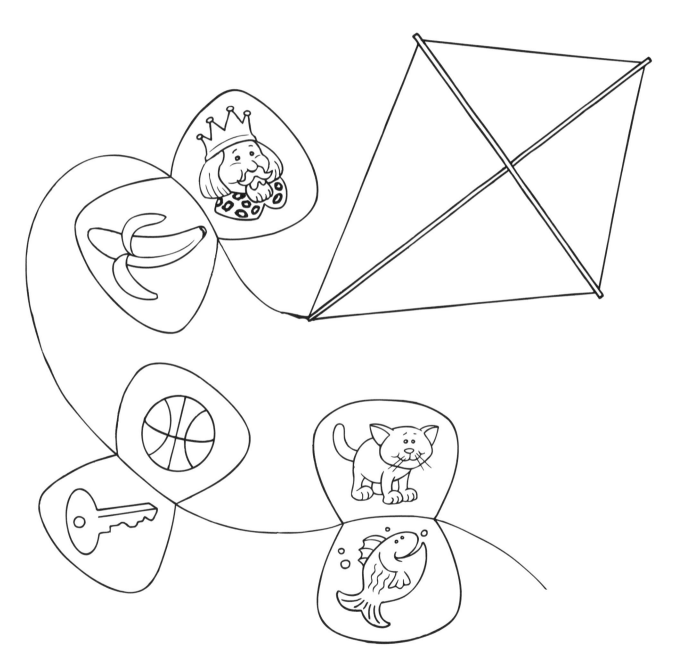

Reading Readiness

BEGINNING CONSONANT Ll

Name: _____

These pictures begin with the letter **Ll**. Color these pictures.

lion

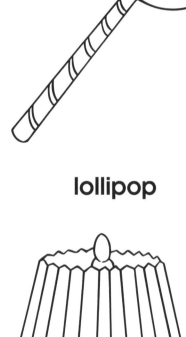

lollipop

lamb

lamp

BEGINNING CONSONANT Ll

Name: _____

Cut out the stamps at the bottom of the page. Say each picture name. If the picture begins with the same sound as **letter**, glue it on an envelope.

Name: _____

Say each picture name. Say each letter. Draw a line from each picture to its beginning letter sound.

J j

K k

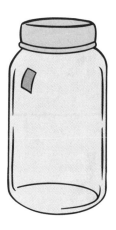

L l

Reading Readiness

BEGINNING SOUNDS
Jj, Kk, Ll

Say the sound the letters make.
Circle the pictures in each row
that begin with the letter shown.

Jj	jump rope	jar	star
Jj	clock	jack-in-the-box	pig
Kk	astronaut	key	kite
Kk	kangaroo	beet	fish
Ll	leaf	fan	log
Ll	lock	lion	lamp

BEGINNING CONSONANT Mm

Name: _____

These pictures begin with the letter **Mm**.
Color these pictures.

moon

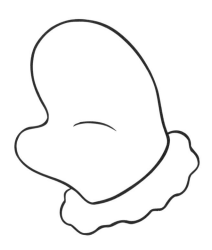

mitten

milk

moose

Reading Readiness

Name: _____

Say each picture name. Color the pictures whose names begin with the same sound as **macaroni** and **meatballs**.

These pictures begin with the letter **Nn**.
Color these pictures.

nine

nest

newspaper

newt

BEGINNING CONSONANT
Nn

Help the birds find their nest. Follow the path with the pictures whose names begin with the same sound as **nest**.

Name:_____

These pictures begin with the letter **Oo**.
Color these pictures.

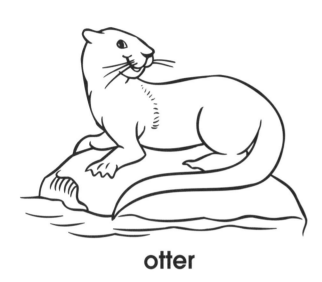

otter

octopus

ox

ostrich

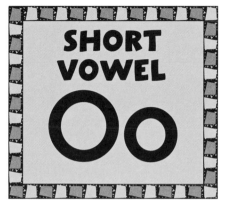
SHORT VOWEL Oo

Short Oo is the sound at the beginning of the word **octopus**. Say each picture name. Color the socks that have the **short Oo** sound. Does this octopus have enough colored socks?_____

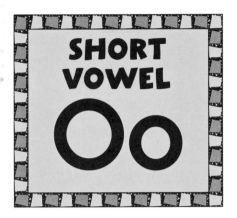

SHORT VOWEL
Oo

Look at the pictures. Color the pictures that begin with the **short Oo** sound.

SHORT VOWEL Oo

Write the letter **o** to complete each word. Read the words. Then find the pictures of the words at the bottom of the page and circle them.

f o x

l o g

d o g

fr o g

Name: _____

Say each picture name. Write **o** to complete each word below.

r __ ck

p __ t

x

b __ x

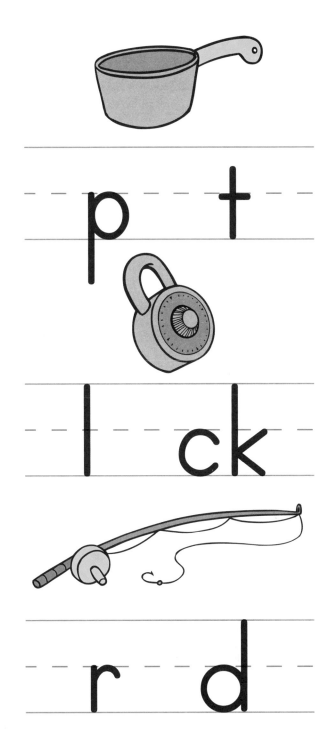

p __ t

l __ ck

r __ d

Reading Readiness

SHORT VOWEL Oo

Name: _____

Say each picture name. Say each word. Draw a line from each picture to the word that names the picture.

cot

tot

pot

Make a flip book to read words. Cut out the cards. Put the big card with the word **cot** on the bottom. Put the letter cards on top of the big card.

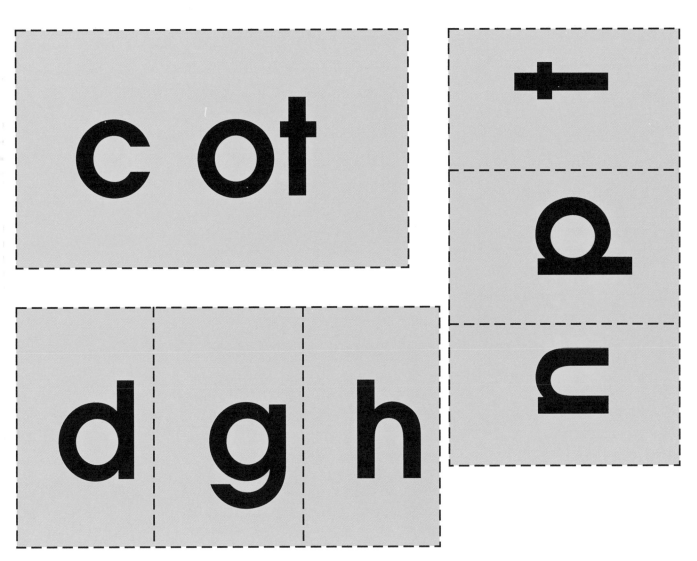

◆ Staple the cards on the far left side.
◆ Then flip the cards and read each word.

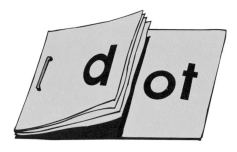

Name:_____

Say each picture name. Cut out the words. Glue each word where it belongs.

hat | pot | hen | fin | mat

BEGINNING SOUNDS
Mm, Nn, Oo

Say the sound the letters make.
Circle the pictures in each row
that begin with the letter shown.

Mm			
Mm			
Nn			
Nn			
Oo			
Oo			

Name: _____

These pictures begin with the letter **Pp**.
Color these pictures.

pin

pig

pie

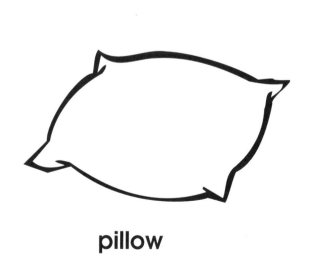

pillow

BEGINNING CONSONANT
Pp

Pam only packs things whose names begin with the same sound as **panda**. Say the picture names. Circle each picture whose name begins with the same sound as **Pam** and **panda**.

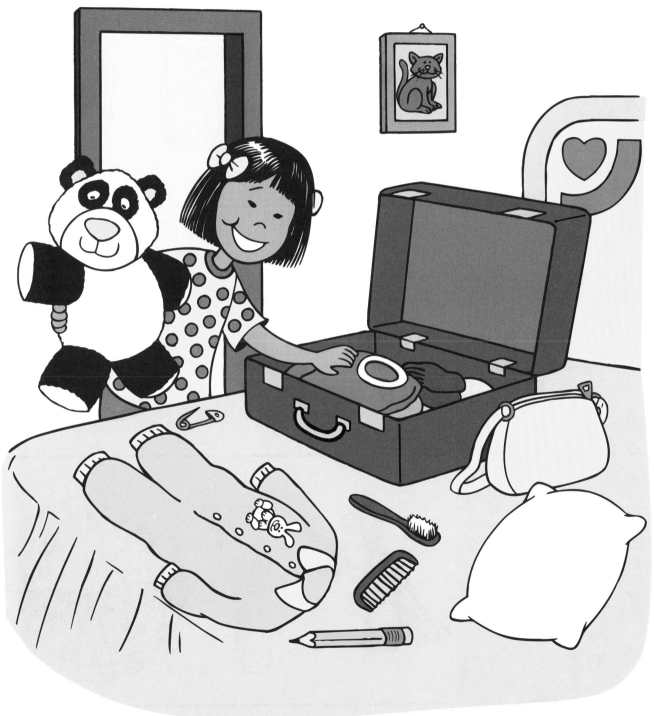

Name: _____

Say the sound the letters make. Circle the pictures in each row that begin with the letter shown.

Mm

  (mermaid)

Nn

Pp

  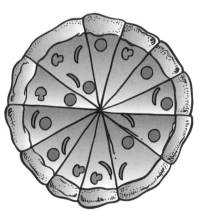

BEGINNING CONSONANT Qq

Name: _____

These pictures begin with the letter **Qq**. Color these pictures.

queen

quilt

quail

quiet

BEGINNING CONSONANT
Qq

Name: _____

Look at the pictures on the quilt below. Say each picture name. If the picture begins with the same sound as **quilt**, color the square yellow. Color the other squares purple.

BEGINNING CONSONANT Rr

These pictures begin with the letter **Rr**.
Color these pictures.

ring

rocket

rabbit

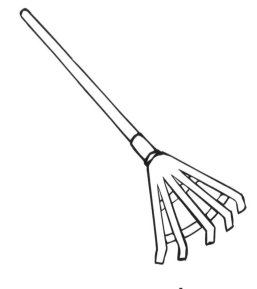

rake

Name: _____

Who is the raccoon going to visit? Say each picture name. Color the pictures whose names begin with the same sound as **raccoon**.

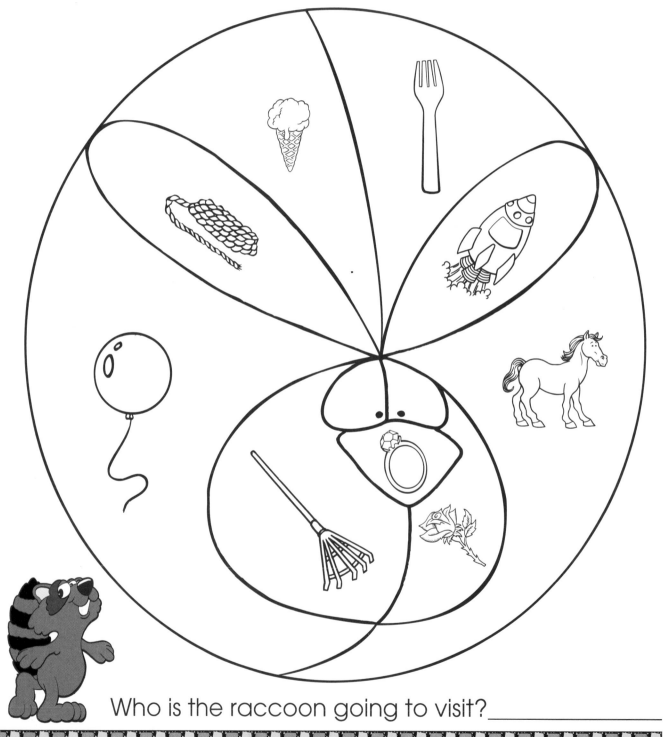

Who is the raccoon going to visit? _____

Name: _____

Say the sound the letters make. Circle the pictures in each row that begin with the letter shown.

Pp			
Pp			
Qq			
Qq			
Rr	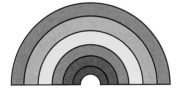		
Rr			

Reading Readiness

BEGINNING CONSONANT
Ss

Name: _____

These pictures begin with the letter **Ss**. Color these pictures.

snowman

sun

scissors

sock

BEGINNING CONSONANT Ss

Name: _____

Find the letter **S**. Say each picture name. If the picture begins with the same sound as **six**, color the space blue. Color the other spaces orange.

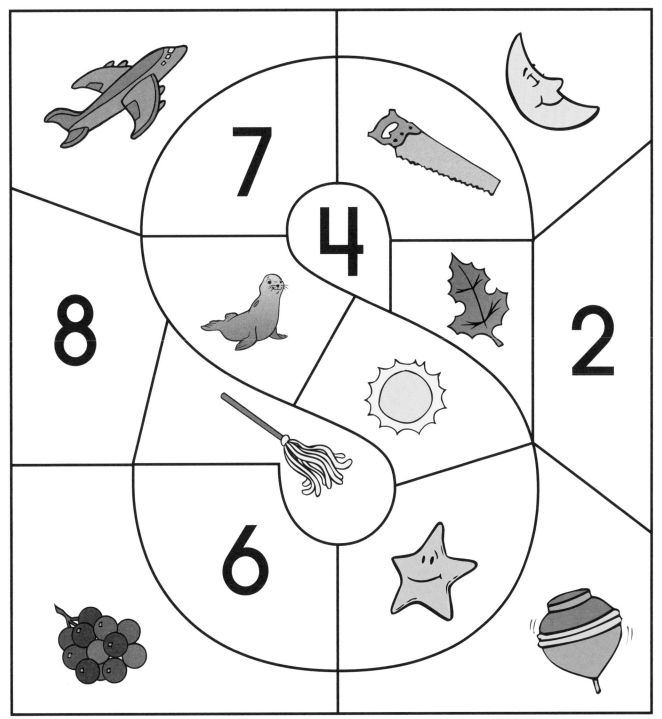

Reading Readiness

Name:_____

Say each picture name. Say the letters. Draw a line from each picture to its matching letter.

Qq

Rr

Ss

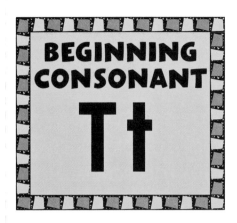

BEGINNING CONSONANT T t

These pictures begin with the letter **Tt**.
Color these pictures.

turtle

tie

table

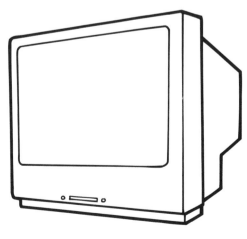

television

BEGINNING CONSONANT
Tt

Say the picture name for each toy in the tub. Draw an **X** on the pictures whose names begin with the same sound as **tub**.

SHORT VOWEL Uu

Name: _____

These pictures begin with the letter **Uu**.
Color these pictures.

umbrella

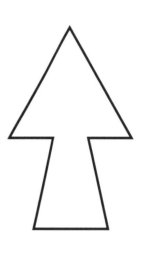

up

umpire

under

SHORT VOWEL Uu

Name: _____

Short Uu is the sound at the beginning of the word **umbrella**. Cut out the pictures at the bottom of the page. Say each picture name. If the picture has the **short Uu** sound, glue it on the umbrella.

SHORT VOWEL Uu

Name: _____

Short Uu is the sound you hear in the middle of the word **bug**. Help the bug get to the leaf. Follow the path with the pictures whose names have the **short Uu** sound.

Reading Readiness

Name: _____

Write the letter **u** to complete each word. Read the word. Draw a line to match each word with its picture.

g___m

c___p

b___g

d___ck

SHORT VOWEL Uu

Short Uu is the sound you hear in the middle of the word **bus**. Say each picture name. Write **u** to complete each word below.

b __ s

h __ g

tr __ ck

m __ d

SHORT VOWEL Uu

Look at the pictures and read the words. Draw a line from each picture to the word that matches it.

cup   **bus**   **gum**   **mug**

SHORT VOWEL Uu

Cut out the wheels. Put the little wheel on top of the big wheel. Push a toothpick through the center. Turn the little wheel. How many words can you make?

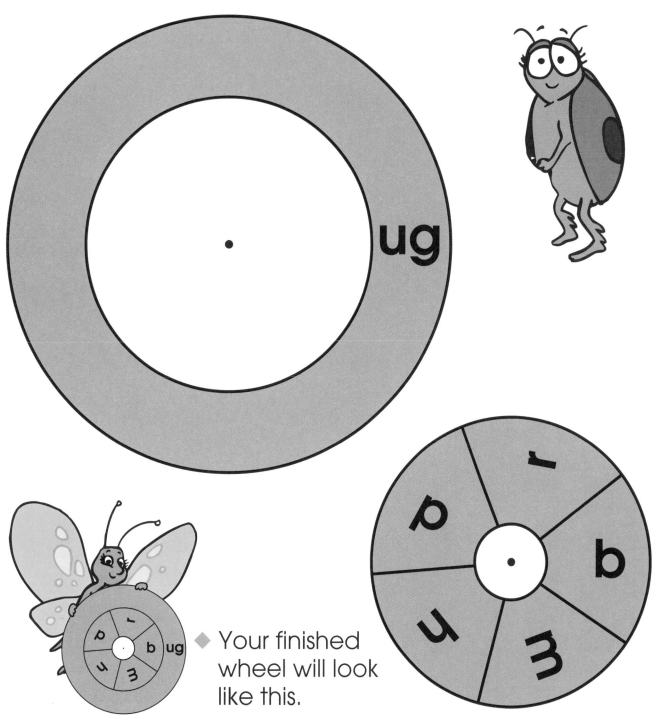

ug

◆ Your finished wheel will look like this.

Reading Readiness

Name: _____

Say the sound the letters make. Circle the pictures in each row that begin with the letter shown.

Ss			
Ss			
Tt			
Tt			
Uu			
Uu			

BEGINNING CONSONANT Vv

Name: _____

These pictures begin with the letter **Vv**.
Color these pictures.

valentine

vase

vacuum

violin

BEGINNING CONSONANT Vv

Cut out the pictures at the bottom of the page. Say each picture name. If the picture begins with the same sound as **van**, glue it on the van.

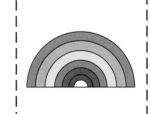    

BE MINE

Reading Readiness

BEGINNING CONSONANT Ww

These pictures begin with the letter **Ww**.
Color these pictures.

wagon

watch

watermelon

window

Name: _____

Say the sound the letters make.
Circle the pictures in each row
that begin with the letter shown.

Tt

Vv

Ww

CONSONANT
Xx

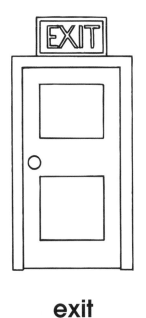

Name: _____

These pictures have the letter **Xx** in them. Color these pictures.

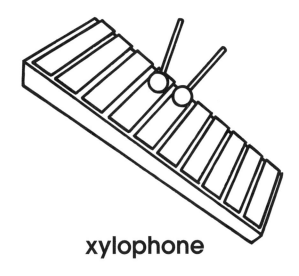

xylophone

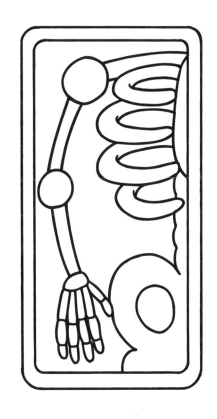

x-ray

exit

CONSONANT
Xx

Write an **x** on the lines to complete each picture name. Then color the big **X**.

_e _it

_-ray

X

b o _

fo _

Name: _____

Say the sound the letters make. Circle the pictures in each row that have the letter shown.

Vv			
Vv			
Ww			
Ww			
Xx			
Xx			

Reading Readiness

BEGINNING CONSONANT
Yy

Name: _____

These pictures begin with the letter **Yy**.
Color these pictures.

yarn

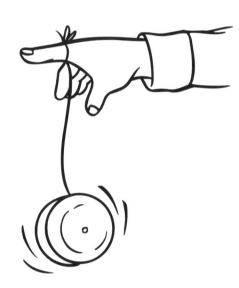

yo-yo

yolk

yak

BEGINNING CONSONANT Yy

Say each picture name. Draw a green line from each ball of yarn to the pictures that begin with the **Yy** sound.

Name: _____

These pictures begin with the letter **Zz**.
Color these pictures.

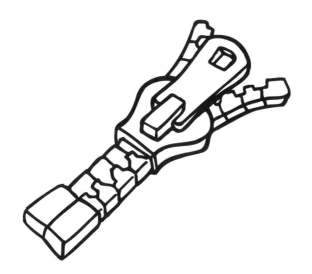

zipper

zig zag

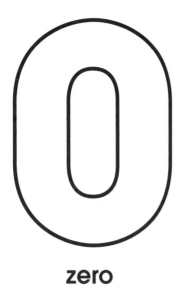

zero

zebra

BEGINNING CONSONANT Zz

The word zero begins with the letter **Zz**. Complete the picture of the zero below.

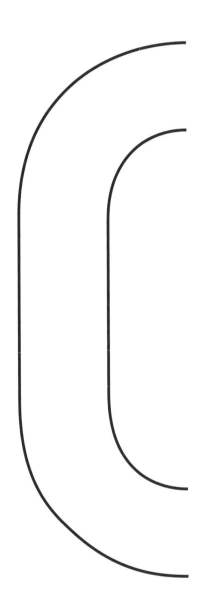

zero

Name: _____

Say the sound the letters make. Circle the pictures in each row that begin with the letter shown.

Xx

Yy

Zz

BEGINNING SOUNDS
Yy, Zz

Say the sound the letters make. Circle the pictures in each row that begin with the letter shown.

Yy		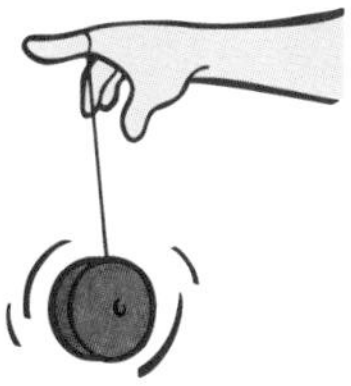	
Yy			Yogurt
Zz			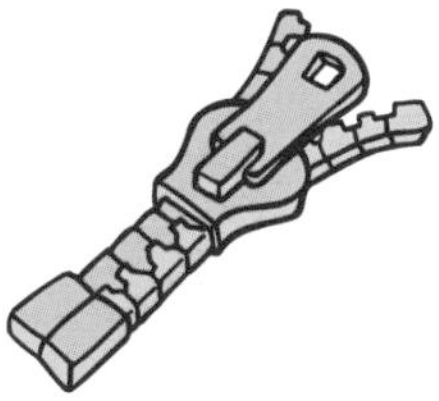
Zz			0

Reading Readiness

Say each picture name. Circle the letter that stands for the beginning sound.

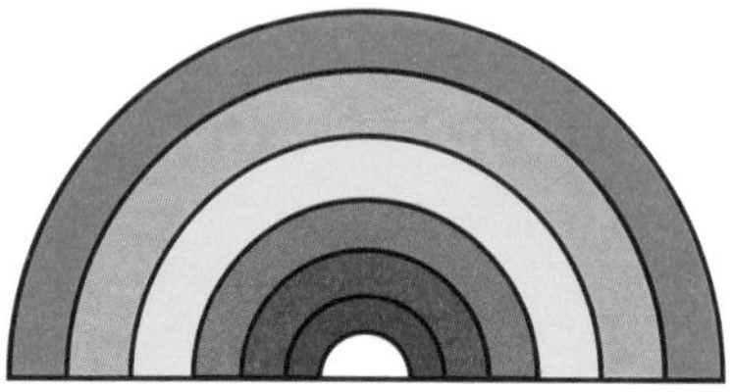 r　　n	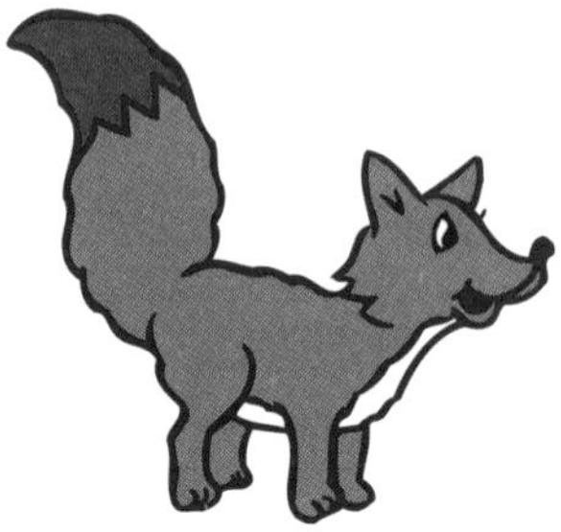 m　　f	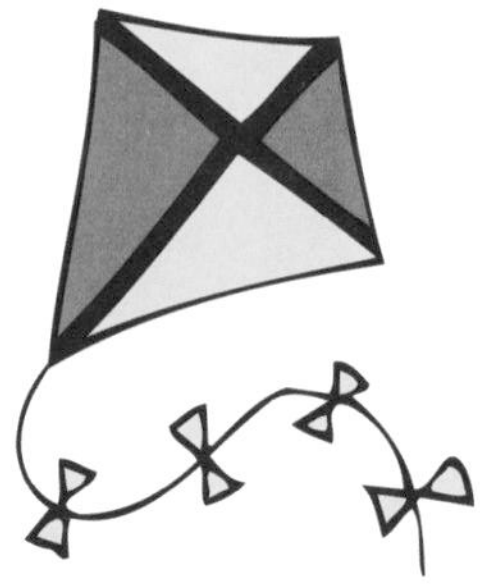 k　　b
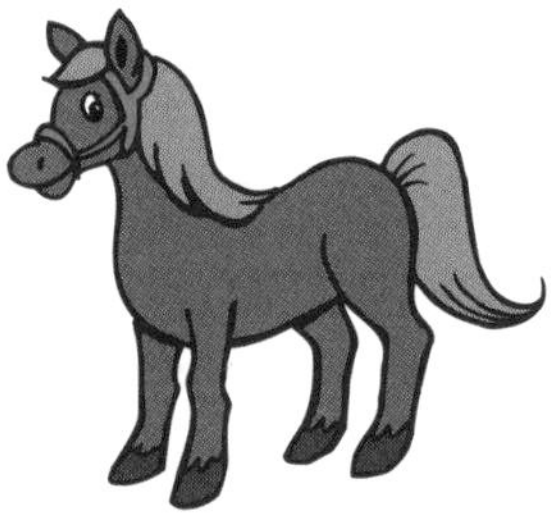 l　　h	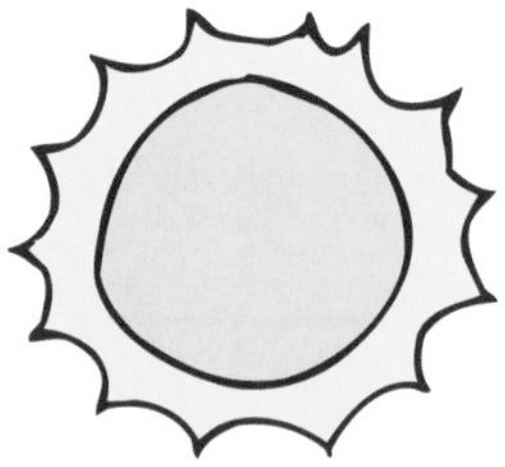 s　　w	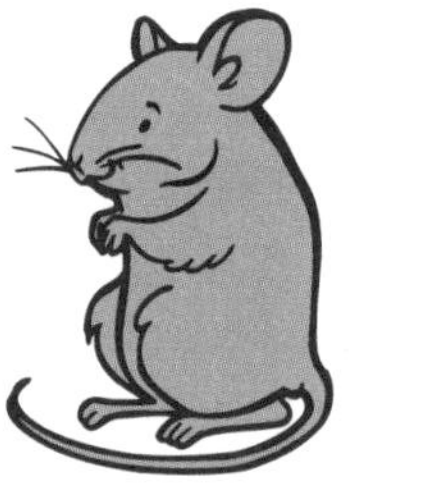 d　　m
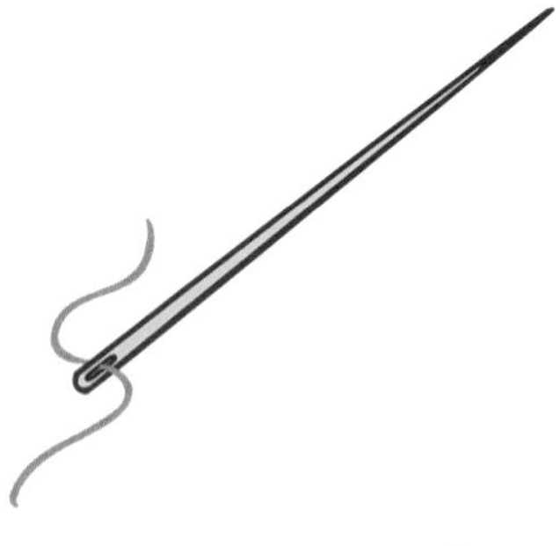 n　　d	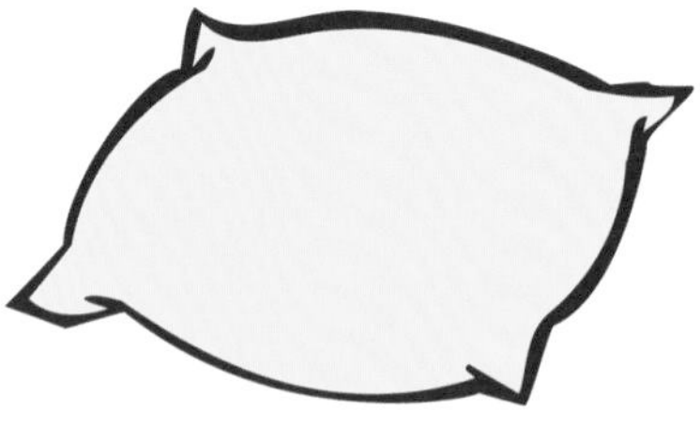 l　　p	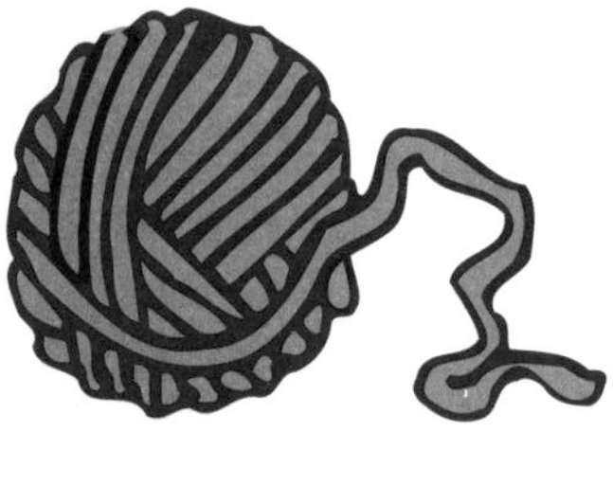 y　　w

REVIEW BEGINNING CONSONANTS

Say each picture name. Circle the beginning sound.

 t　p	 n　c	 b　t
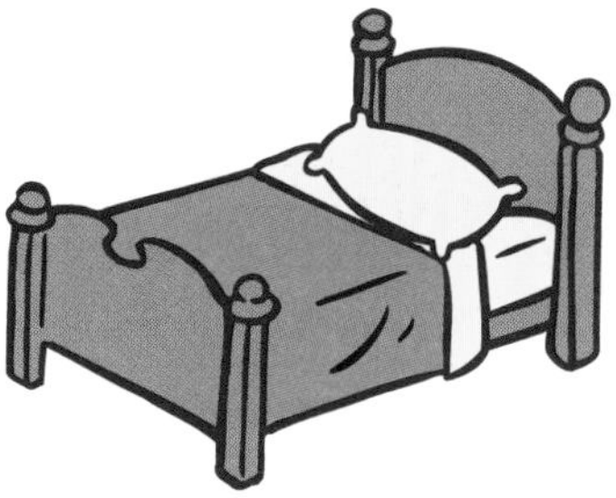 b　c	 t　p	 c　b
 c　t	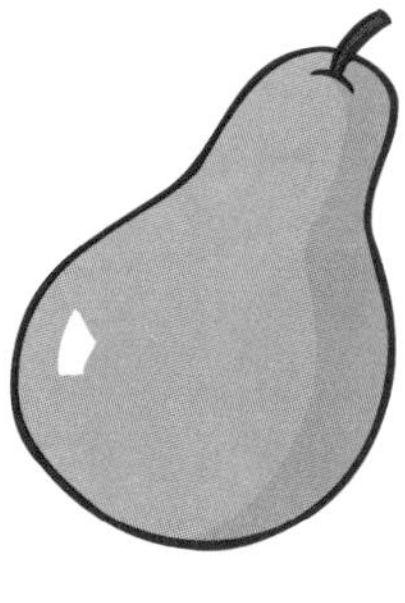 b　p	 p　n

Name: _____

REVIEW BEGINNING CONSONANTS

Say each picture name. Circle the beginning sound.

p t	b p	n c
n b	t n	t b
p b	c p	c b

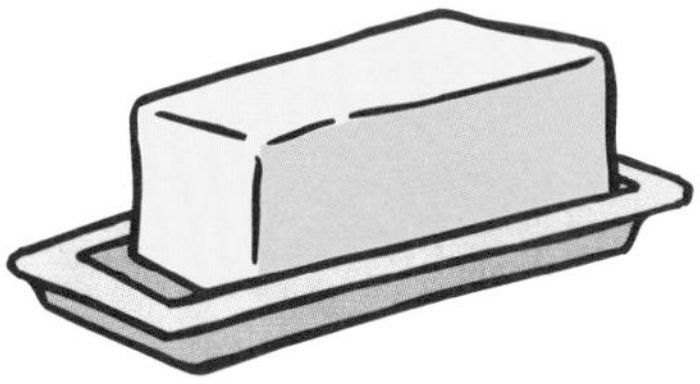

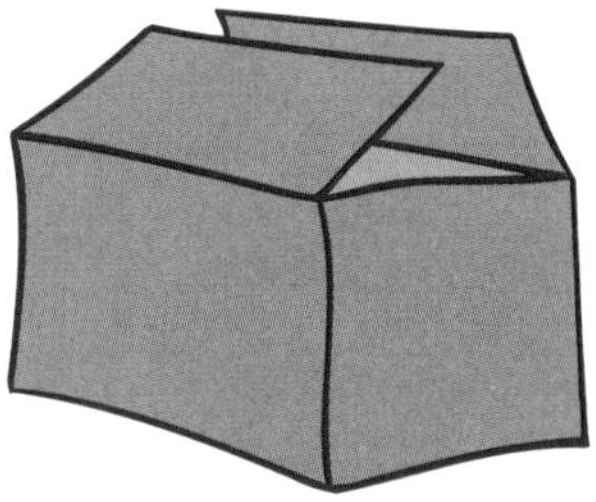

BEGINNING CONSONANTS

Say the sound the letter makes.
Circle the pictures in each row
that begin with the letter shown.

b

c

t

n

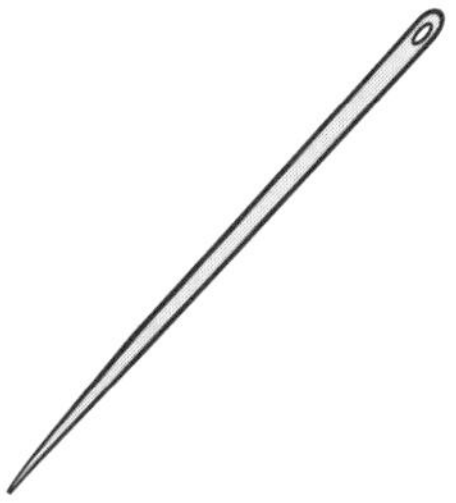

Reading Readiness

REVIEW
BEGINNING CONSONANTS

Name: _____

Look at the letter in each box. Circle the picture that begins with that sound.

REVIEW BEGINNING CONSONANTS

Name: _____

Look at the letter in each column. Cut out each picture and glue it under the correct beginning sound.

Hh	Dd	Rr	Gg

Reading Readiness

Name: _____

Look at the letter in each column.
Cut out each picture and glue it
under the correct beginning sound.

Mm	Ll	Ss	Pp

Name: _____

Look at each picture. Write the beginning sound for each picture.

_____

- - - - - - - - - - - -

_____

_____

- - - - - - - - - - - -

_____

_____

- - - - - - - - - - - -

_____

_____

- - - - - - - - - - - -

_____

_____

- - - - - - - - - - - -

_____

_____

- - - - - - - - - - - -

_____

_____

- - - - - - - - - - - -

_____

_____

- - - - - - - - - - - -

_____

_____

- - - - - - - - - - - -

_____

Name: _____

Look at each picture. Write the beginning sound for each picture.

_____

_____

_____

_____

_____

_____

Name: _____

Look at the picture in each box.
Color the pictures in that row with
the same beginning sound.

Reading Readiness

Name: _____

Look at each pair of pictures. Circle the pairs that begin with the same sound.

Name: _____

Look at each pair of pictures.
Circle the pairs that begin with
the same sound.

Reading Readiness

Name: _____

Look at the pictures. Draw a line to match pictures with the same beginning sound.

Cut out the letters and pictures below and on pages 289–293. Mix them up and turn them over to match the beginning sound with its picture.

Aa	Bb	Cc
Dd	Ee	Ff
Gg	Hh	Ii
Jj	Kk	Ll
Mm	Nn	Oo

BEGINNING SOUND MEMORY GAME

Pp	Qq	Rr
Ss	Tt	Uu
Vv	Ww	Xx
Yy	Zz	

BEGINNING SOUND MEMORY GAME

BEGINNING SOUND MEMORY GAME

ENDING CONSONANT SOUNDS

Name: _____

Look at the picture in each box. Color the pictures in that row that end with the same sound.

Reading Readiness

ENDING CONSONANT SOUNDS

Look at the picture in each box. Circle the pictures in that row that have the same ending sound.

ENDING CONSONANT SOUNDS

Look at the picture in each box. Circle the ending sound for each picture.

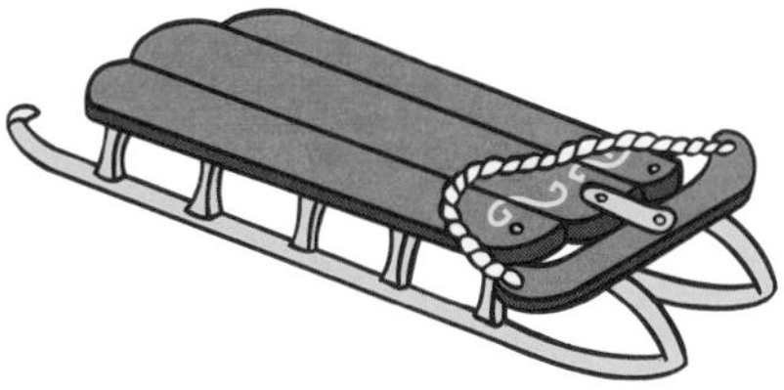

d t	b p	x s
n m	g f	s b
r t	d r	g v

ENDING CONSONANT SOUNDS

Say each picture name. Fill in the circle next to the ending sound.

○ t ○ p	○ n ○ b	○ b ○ t
○ n ○ p	○ p ○ b	○ p ○ t
○ b ○ p	○ n ○ p	○ t ○ n

ENDING CONSONANT SOUNDS

Say the name of each picture.
Write the letter to complete
each word.

ha _____

ja _____

ru _____

pi _____

da _____

re _____

VOWEL SOUNDS

Name: _____

Look at the picture in each box. Circle the pictures in that row that have the same vowel sound.

VOWEL SOUNDS

Look at each picture. Draw a line to the letter that makes the same vowel sound.

a

e

i

o

u

VOWEL SOUNDS

Name: _____

Look at each picture. Draw a line to the letter that makes the same vowel sound.

Say each picture name. Circle
the vowel sound you hear.

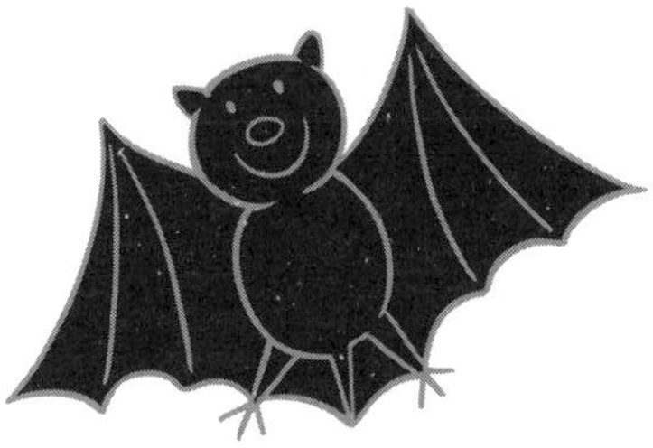 a i	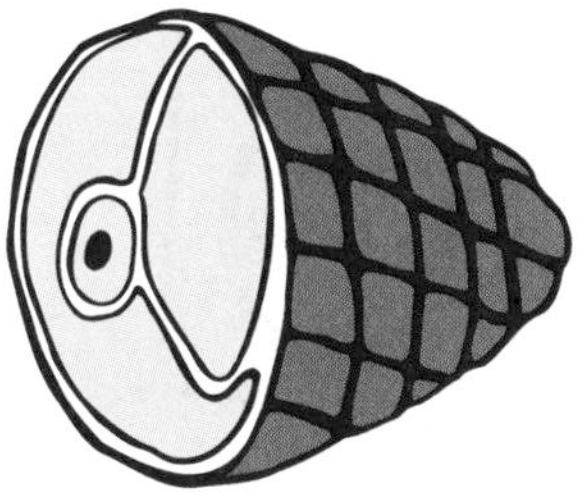 a i	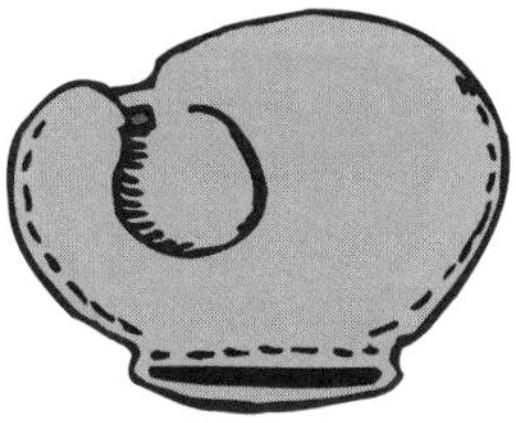 a i
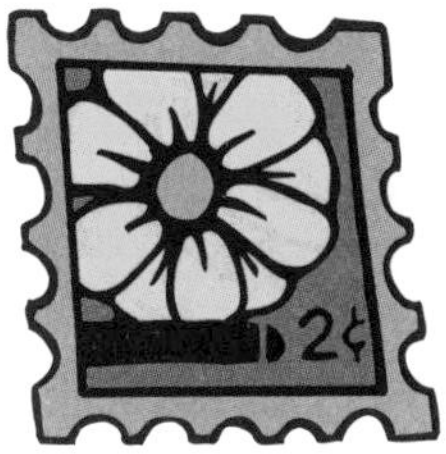 a i	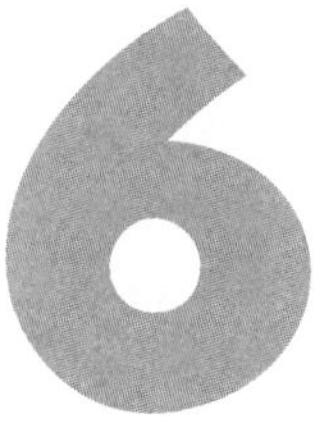 a i	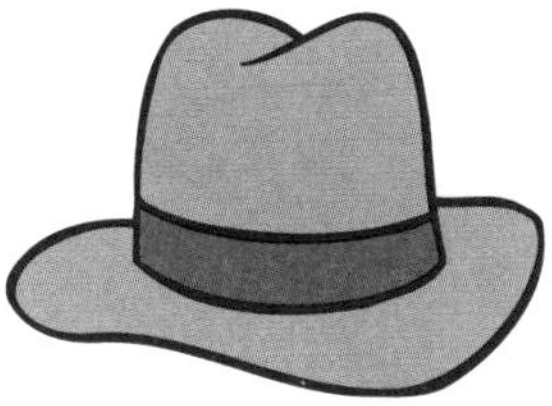 a i
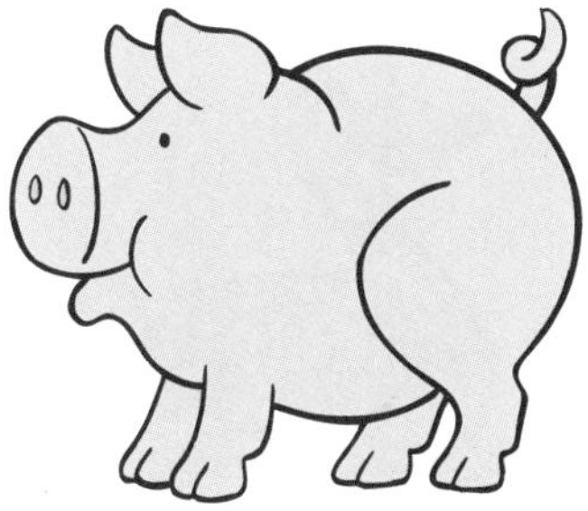 a i	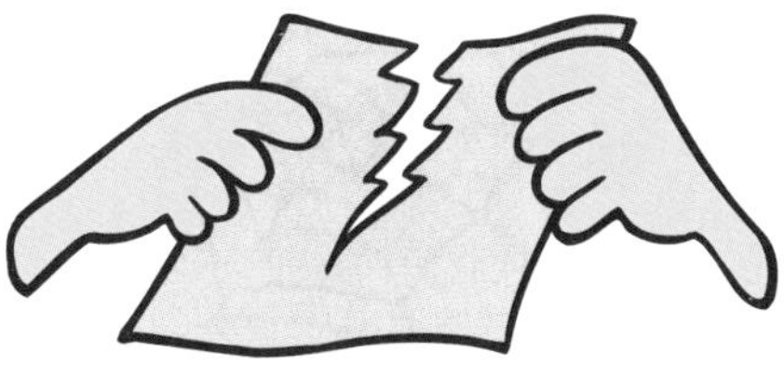 a i	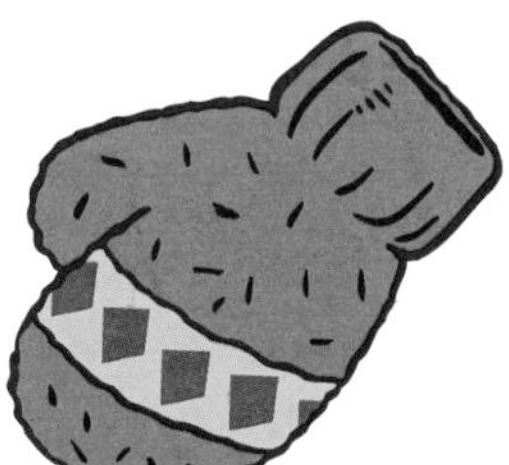 a i

REVIEW
SHORT VOWELS
Oo, Uu, Ee

Name: ______________________________

Say each picture name. Circle the vowel sound you hear.

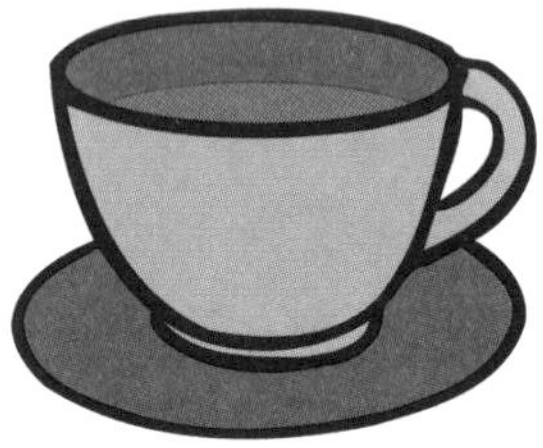

o u e

o u e

o u e

o u e

o u e

o u e

o u e

o u e

o u e

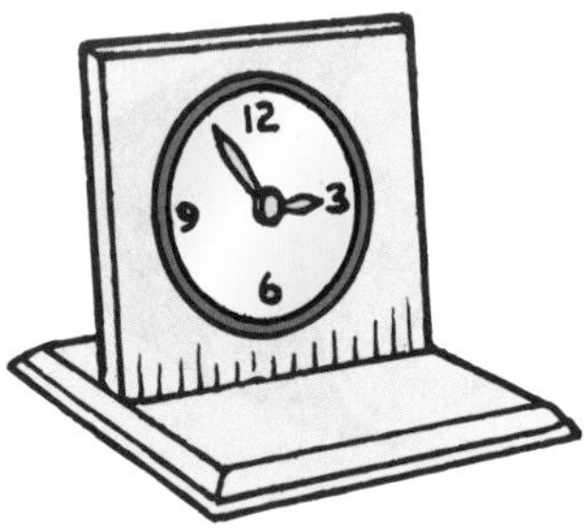

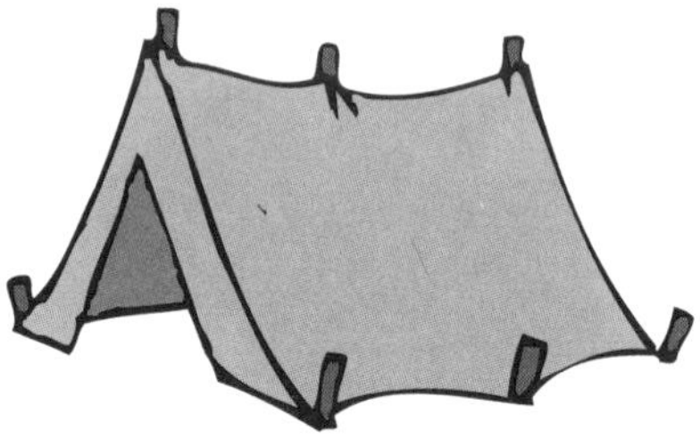

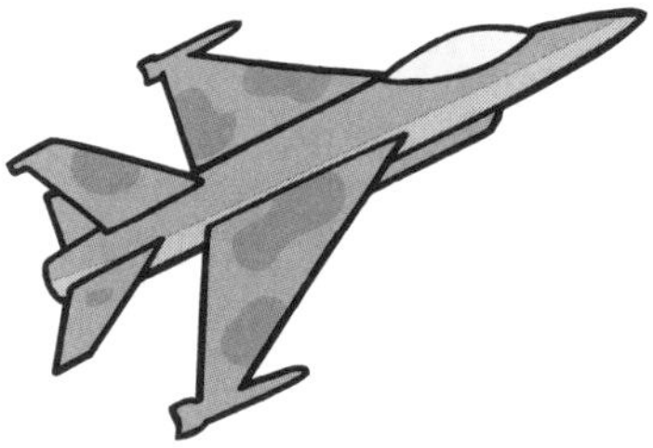

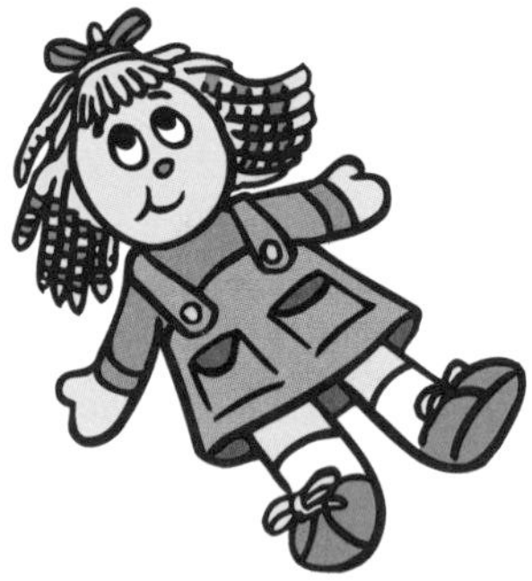

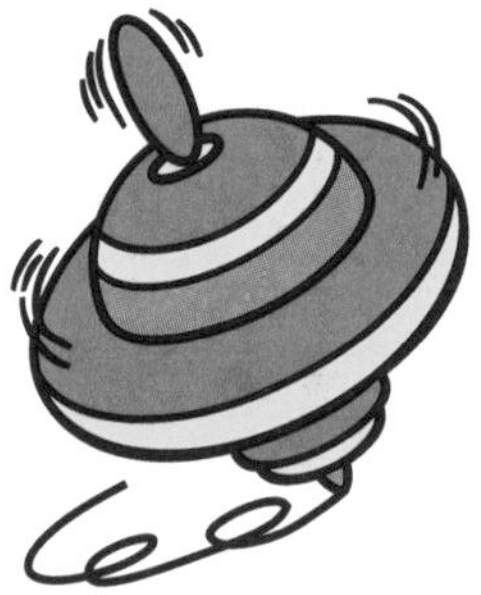

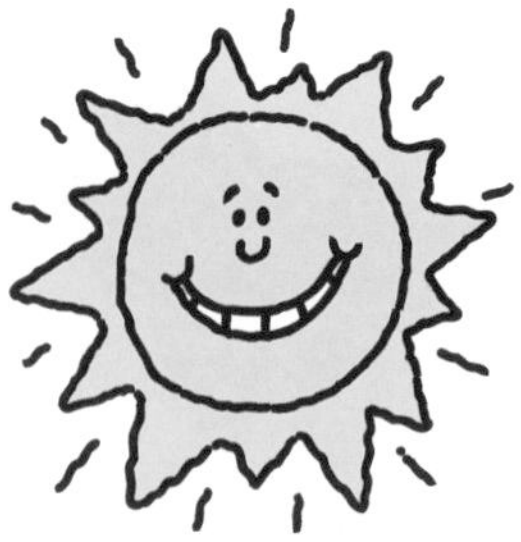

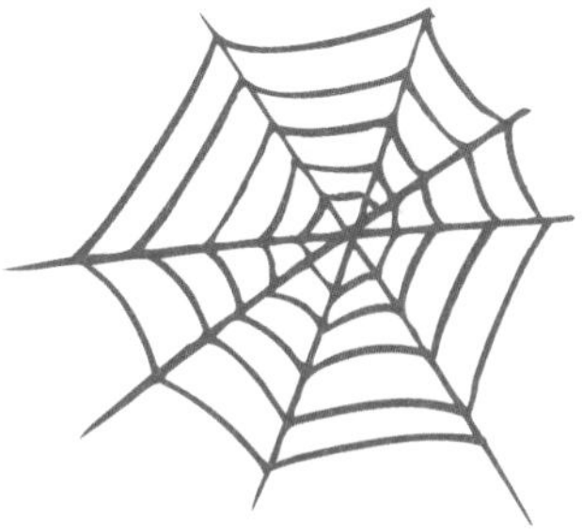

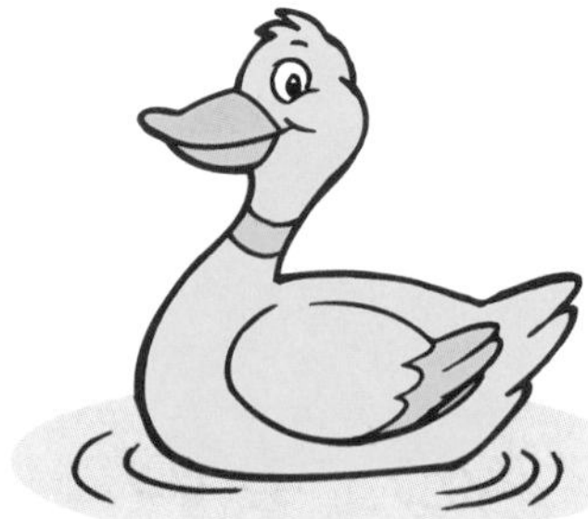

Name: _____

Say the name of each picture. Write the letter to complete each word.

c   p   p   g

d   g   p   n

b   ll   b   d

Name: _____

Find the words in the puzzle and circle them.

b	a	t	h	c	i	t
x	c	c	g	o	k	f
a	y	a	p	o	n	i
r	a	t	j	m	p	l
n	r	i	h	a	t	n

bat   cat   rat   hat

SHORT VOWEL MAZE

Name: _____

Color your way through the maze by only coloring the vowels. Then write the five vowels below.

START ↓

a	b	m	d	t	g	r
e	m	a	u	o	d	p
o	i	e	k	i	i	e
h	n	c	w	r	n	a
u	o	i	b	o	o	u
a	p	i	e	a	f	k
e	a	c	s	y	l	j

END ↓

_____ _____ _____ _____ _____

Name: _____

Write two words with the same short vowel sound to describe the picture.

The _____ is _____ .

The _____ is _____ .

The _____ is _____ .

RHYMING PAIRS

Name: _____

Words that have the same ending sounds are called **rhyming** words. Circle the pairs that rhyme.

map   **nest**   **dog**   **frog**

hat   **bat**   **kite**   **mop**

can   **fan**   **rat**   **pig**

RHYMING PAIRS

Name: _____

Look at each pair of words and pictures. Circle the pairs that rhyme.

 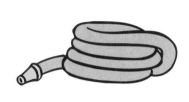  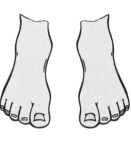

nose   **hose**   **beet**   **feet**

 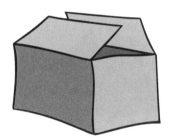 

star   **jar**   **box**   **fox**

dish   **fish**   **cake**   **cap**

Name: _____

Think of a word that rhymes with each picture. Draw a picture. Write the word.

bug

_____

_ _ _ _ _ _ _ _ _ _ _

_____

frog

_____

_ _ _ _ _ _ _ _ _ _ _

_____

RHYMING PAIRS

Name: _____

Think of a word that rhymes with each picture. Draw a picture. Write the word.

cat

pan

RHYME TIME

Name: _____

Read the poem. Read the questions. Circle the correct answer.

Jack and Jill went up the hill,
To fetch a pail of water.
Jack fell down and broke his crown,
And Jill came tumbling after.

◆ Who went up the hill?

◆ What were they going to fetch?

◆ Who fell down?

313

Name: _____

Color each picture the correct color.

red shirt

blue pants

yellow ball

green car

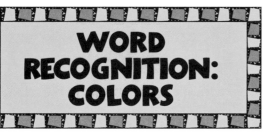
Name: _____

Color each picture the correct color.

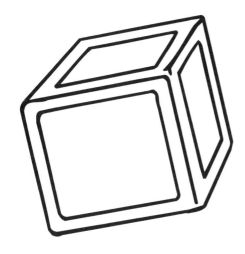

orange block

pink pig

purple balloon

brown bear

WORD RECOGNITION: PEOPLE

Name: ______________________________

Draw a line to match each word with its picture.

boy

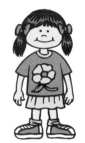

girl

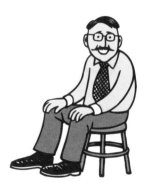

man

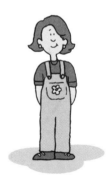

woman

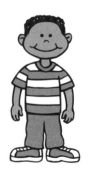

Name: _____

Draw a line to match each word with its picture.

cat

flower

car

tree

WORD RECOGNITION: THINGS

Name: ______________________________

Draw a line to match each word with its picture.

ball

apple

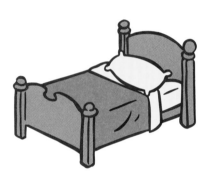

bed

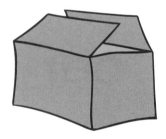

box

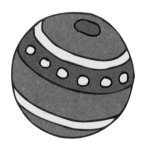

Name:_____

Draw a line to match the action word with the person doing that action.

walk

run

talk

eat

Name: _____

Draw a line to match the action word with the person doing that action.

play

ride

sit

cook

WORD RECOGNITION: DESCRIPTIONS

Name: ______________________________

Draw a line to match each word with its picture.

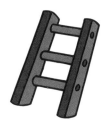

tall

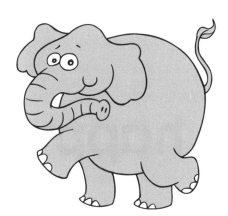

short

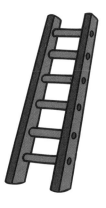

old

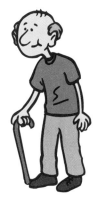

big

Name: _____

Draw a line to match each word with its picture.

little

happy

sad

funny

AFTER

Name: _____

Circle the small picture that shows what will happen after the pictures in the large boxes.

AFTER

Name: _____

Circle the small picture that shows what will happen after the pictures in the large boxes.

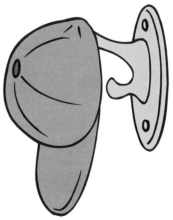

Name: _____

Circle the small picture that shows what will happen after the pictures in the large boxes.

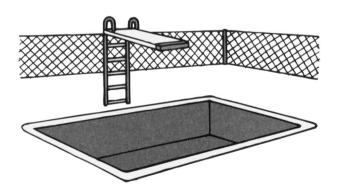

AFTER

Name: _____

Circle the small picture that shows what will happen after the pictures in the large boxes.

BEFORE

Name: _____

Circle the small picture that shows what happened right before the pictures in the large boxes.

BEFORE

Name: _____

Circle the small picture that shows what happened right before the pictures in the large boxes.

Mathematics Readiness

Circle the small picture that shows what happened right before the pictures in the large boxes.

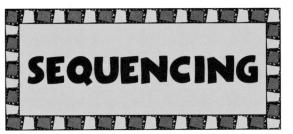

Cut out the pictures below. Put them in the correct order. Draw what you think will happen next.

SEQUENCING

Name: _____

Cut out the pictures below. Put them in the correct order. Draw what you think will happen next.

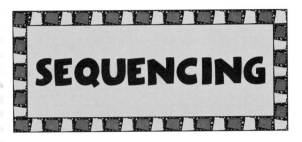

Name: _____

Write numbers in the boxes to show the correct order to tell the story.

FIRST

Name: _____

Look at the pictures in each row. Circle the picture that shows what happened first.

FIRST

Circle the first thing in each row.

Mathematics Readiness

SECOND

Circle the second thing in each row.

  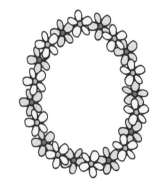 

THIRD

Name: _____

Circle the third thing in each row.

Mathematics Readiness

FIRST, SECOND, THIRD

Name: _____

What happened first, second and third? Draw a line from the correct word to the picture.

first

second

third

SCHOOL BUS STOP

FOURTH

Name: _____

Circle the fourth thing in each row.

Mathematics Readiness

Name:_____

Circle the fifth thing in each row.

ORDINAL NUMBERS

Color the first leaf red. Circle the third leaf.

Color the fourth balloon purple. Draw a line under the second balloon.

Mathematics Readiness

LAST

Circle the last thing in each row.

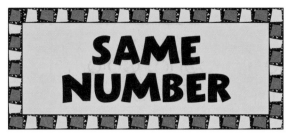

SAME NUMBER

Name: _____

Each pond has the same number of ducks in it. Color the ducks.

Mathematics Readiness

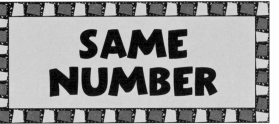

SAME NUMBER

Name: _____

Look at the first pond. Color the same number of ducks in the second pond.

Name: _____

Color the pictures that have the same number of things in each box.

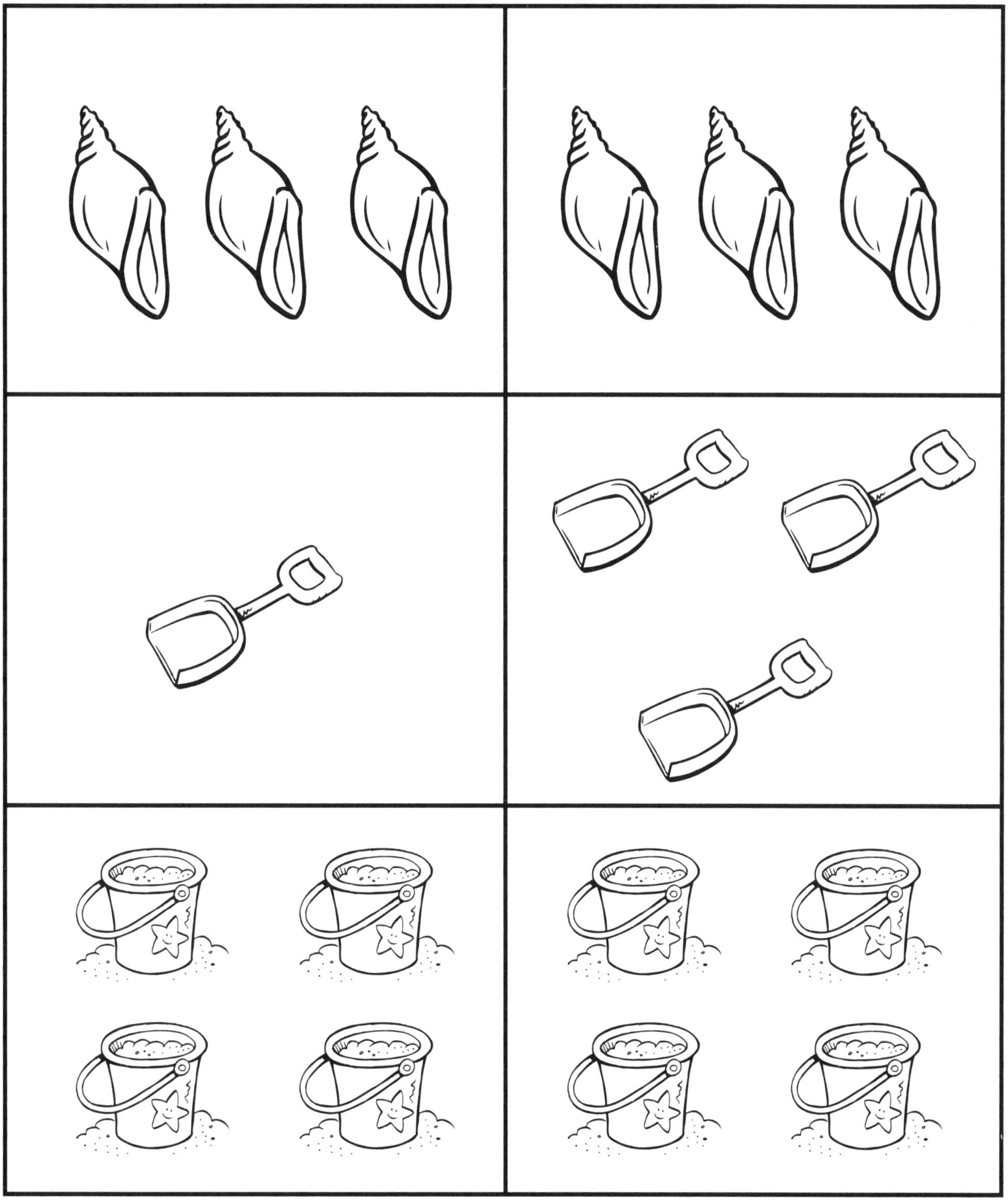

Mathematics Readiness

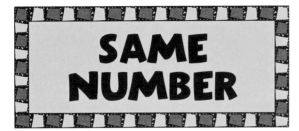

Name: _____

Draw kites so that Sue has the same number as Billy.

ONE FOR EACH

Name: _____

One shoe is correct for each person's job. Draw a line to match each person to the correct shoe.

Mathematics Readiness

ONE FOR EACH

Each animal needs a home.
Draw a line to match each
animal with a home.

Each animal needs a home.
Draw a line to match each
animal with a home.

ONE FOR EACH

Name:_____

Each circus seal needs one ball.
Draw a ball for each seal.

Name: _____

Color the group in each box that has more.

Name: _____

Circle the group in each box that has more.

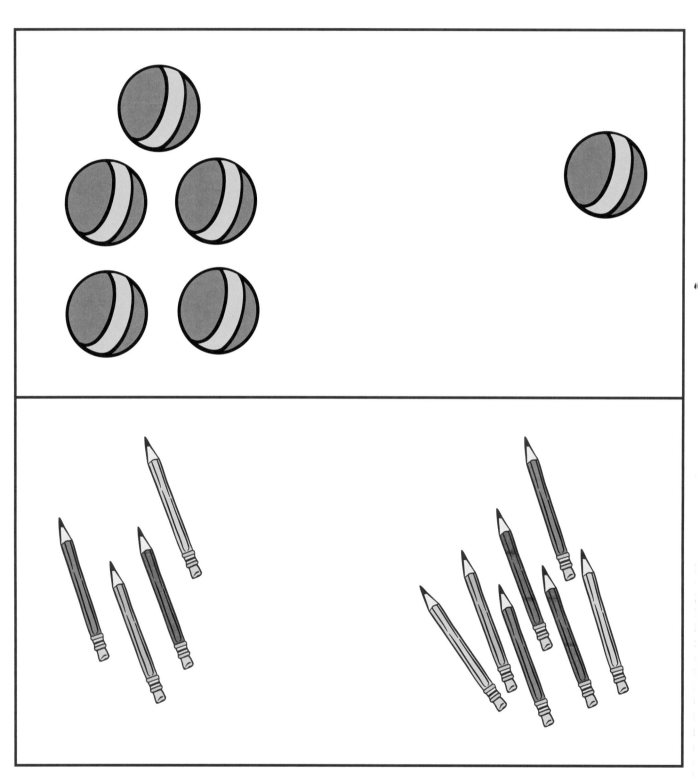

MORE

Circle the group in each box that has more.

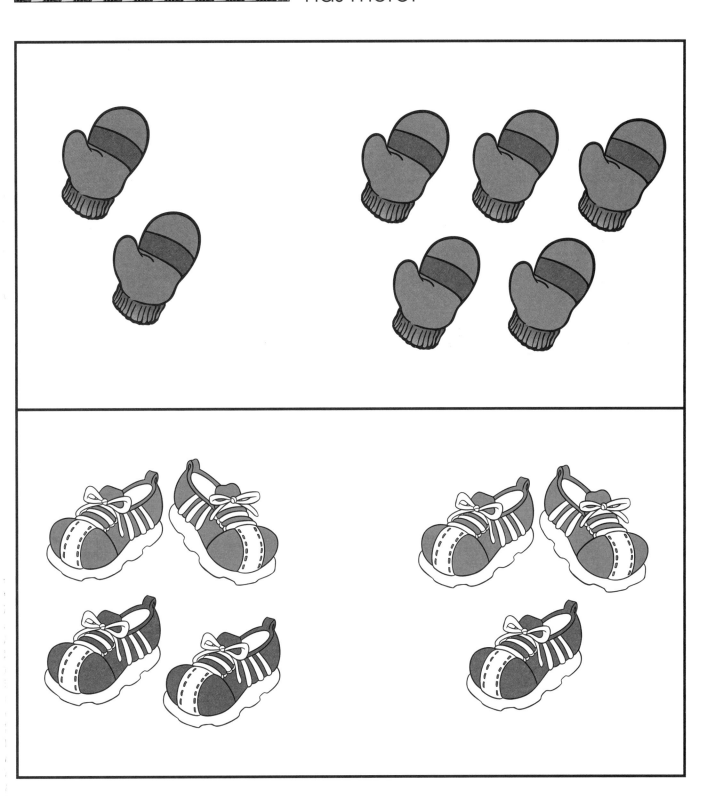

FEWER

Name: _____

Color the group in each box that has fewer.

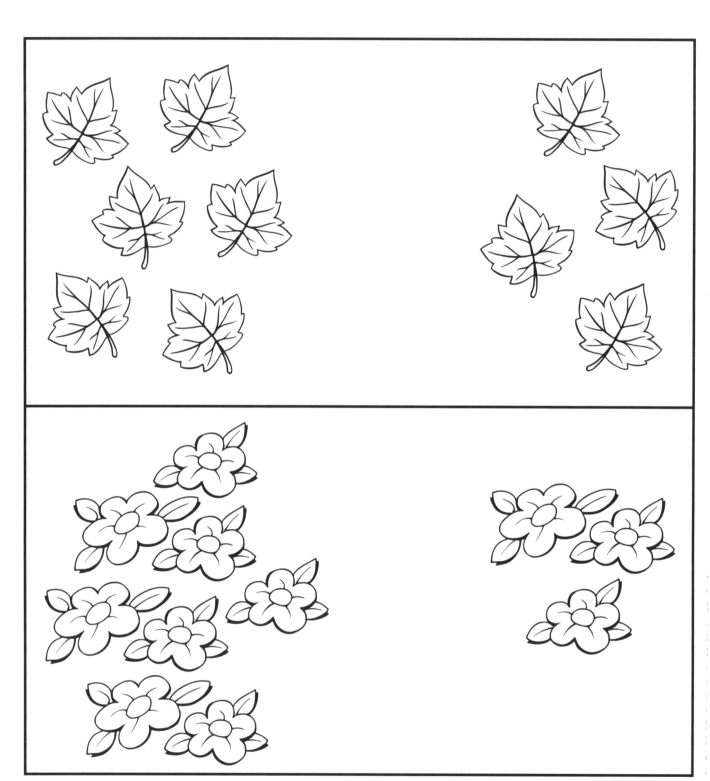

FEWER

Circle the group in each box that has fewer.

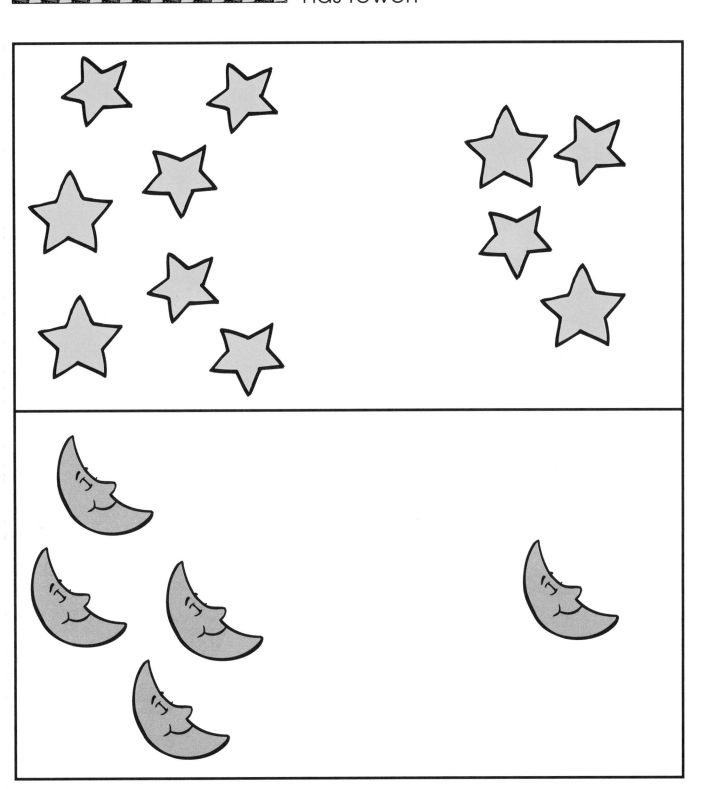

Mathematics Readiness

FEWER

Circle the group in each box that has fewer.

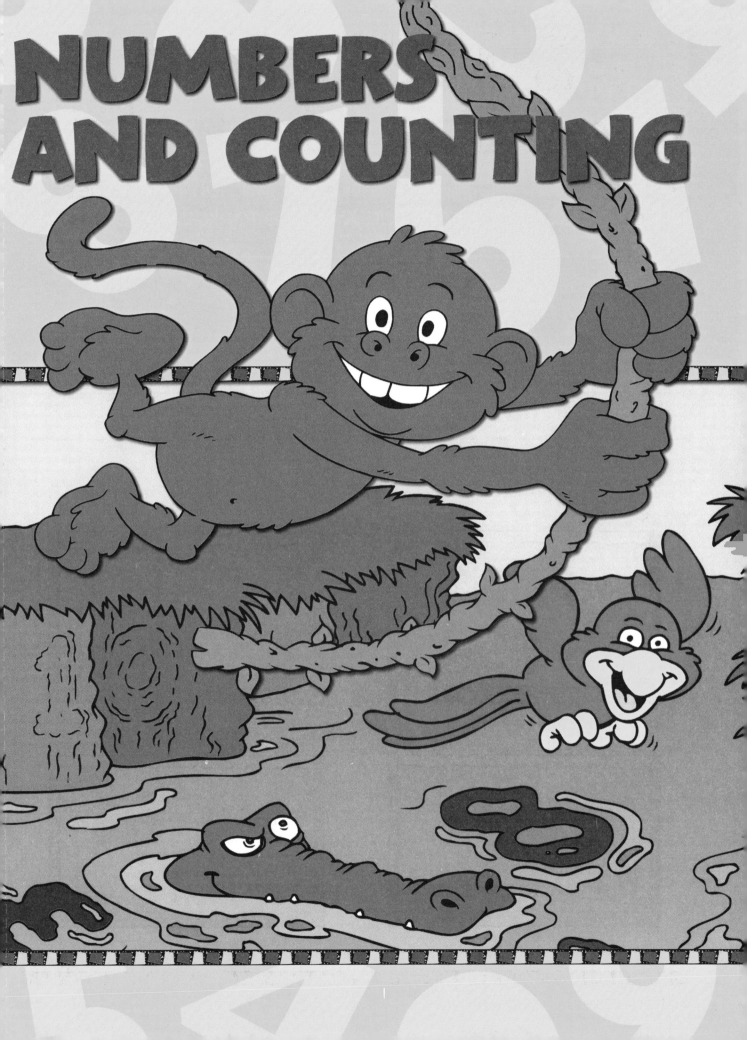

NUMBERS AND COUNTING

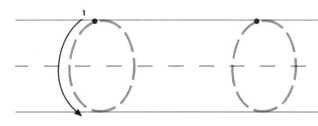

ZERO

0

Name: _____

Trace and write the number **0**. Then draw an **X** on the tanks with zero fish.

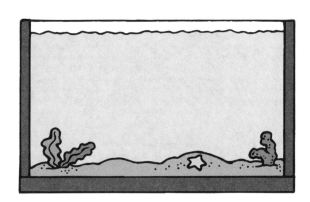

ZERO

0

Trace and write the number word. Then circle the number of fish in each tank.

zero   zero

0   1   3

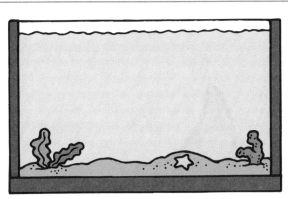

0   1   2

3   4   5

0   1   2

Name: _____

Trace and write the numbers **1** and **2**. Then count and write the correct number.

ONE

1

Name: _____

Trace and write the number word. Then circle each picture that shows one fruit.

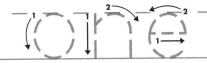 

Numbers and Counting

TWO
2

Name: _____

Trace and write the number word. Help the bunny twins catch their balloons. Follow the twos through the maze.

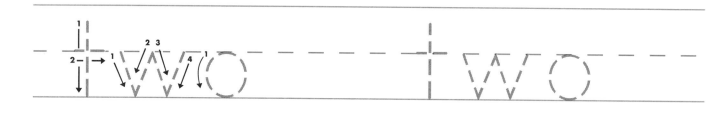

ONE AND TWO

Name: _____

Count and write the number in each box. Circle the groups of one. Color the groups of two.

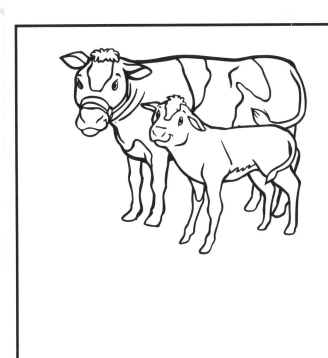

_____

_____

_____

_____

Numbers and Counting

ONE AND TWO

Name: _____

Count and write the number in each box. Circle the groups of one. Color the groups of two.

THREE AND FOUR
3, 4

Trace and write the numbers **3** and **4**. Then count and write the correct number.

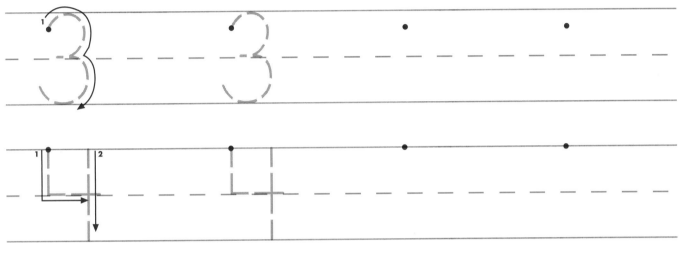

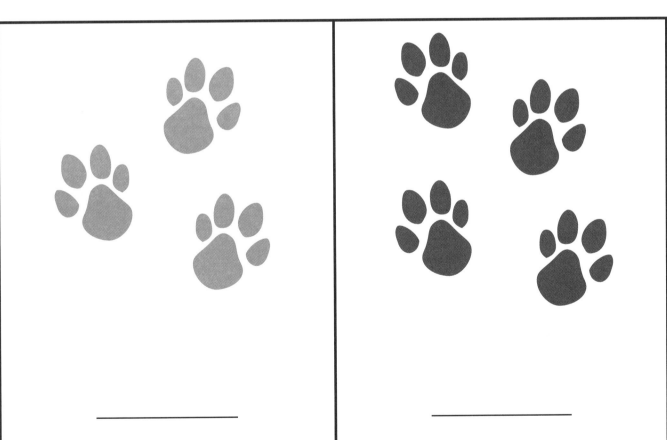

THREE

3

Name: _____

Trace and write the number word.
Under each picture write the number of things.

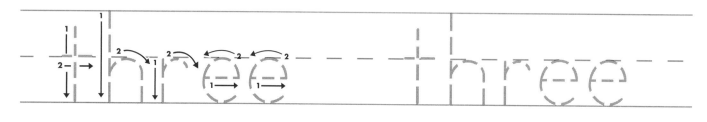

_____   _____   _____

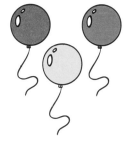

_____   _____   _____

FOUR

4

Name: _____

Trace and write the number word. Then complete the picture by drawing four fish and four seagulls.

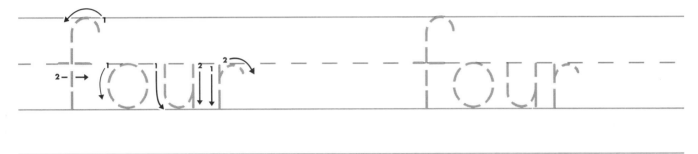

Numbers and Counting

Name: _____

Count and write the number in each box. Circle the groups of three. Color the groups of four.

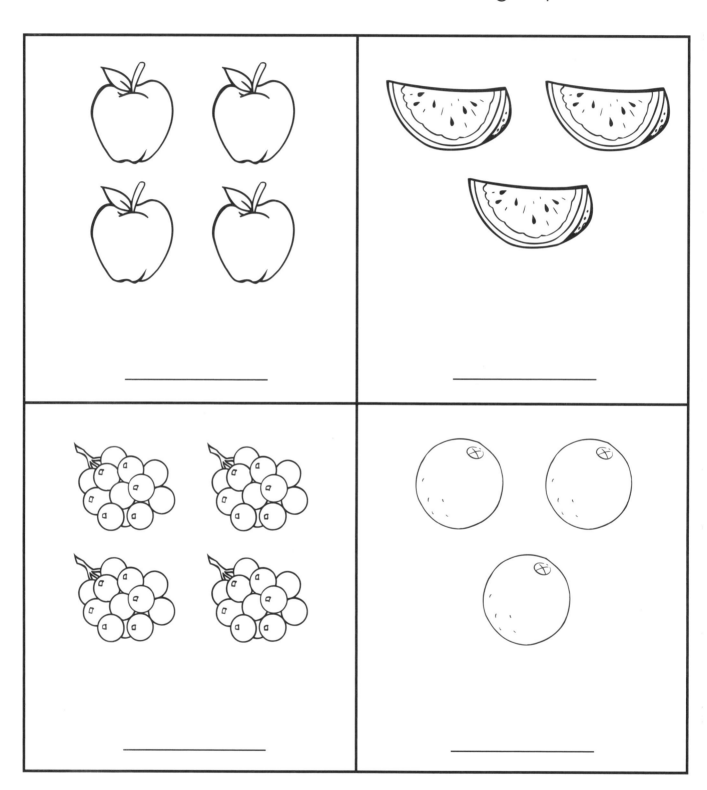

Name: _____

Count and write the number in each box. Circle the groups of three. Color the groups of four.

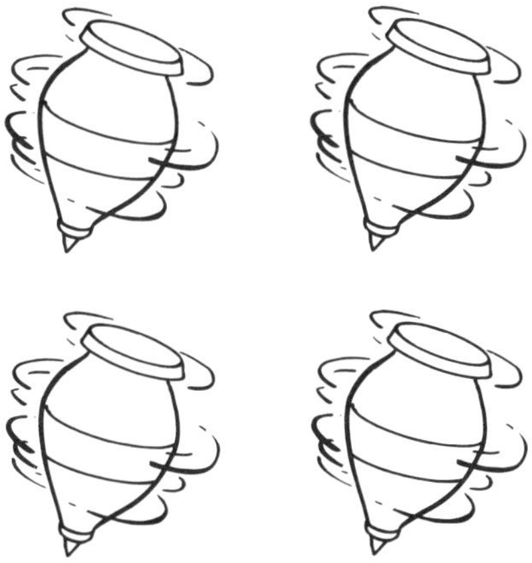

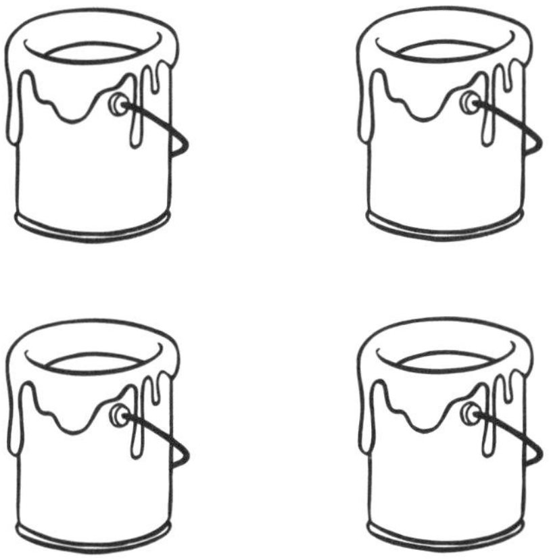

FIVE
5

Name: _____

Trace and write the number **5**.

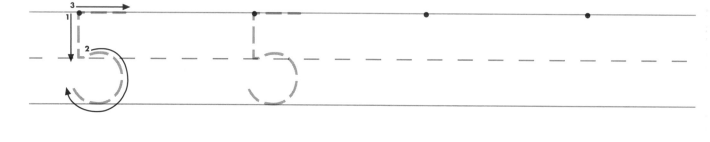

◆ 5 dogs are colored.

◆ Color five dogs.

Name: _____

Trace and write the number word. Write the correct number on each domino.

Name: _____

Look at the picture. Read the questions.
Circle the correct number.

◆ How many in all?   1   2   3

◆ How many in all?   1   2   3

◆ How many in all?   2   3   4

Name: _____

Look at the picture. Read the questions.
Circle the correct number.

◆ How many in all?   3   4   5

◆ How many in all?   3   4   5

◆ How many in all?   3   4   5

REVIEW NUMBERS 1-5

Count the balloons, then write the correct number on the line.

_____

_____

_____

_____   _____

Name: _____

Connect the dots in order. Color the picture.

◆ Trace the numbers below. Then write the missing numbers.

2   4

REVIEW NUMBERS 1 - 5

Draw a line from the number to the group that matches.

1

2

3

4

5

SIX

6

Name: _____

Trace and write the number **6**. Then draw 6 coins in the piggy bank.

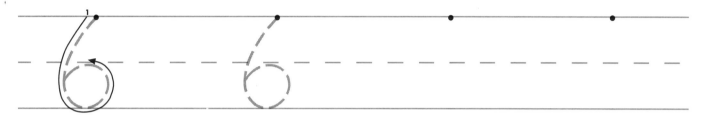

SIX
6

Trace and write the number word.
Draw an **X** on each group of six things.

Name: _____

Count and write the number in each box. Circle the groups of five. Draw an **X** on the groups of six.

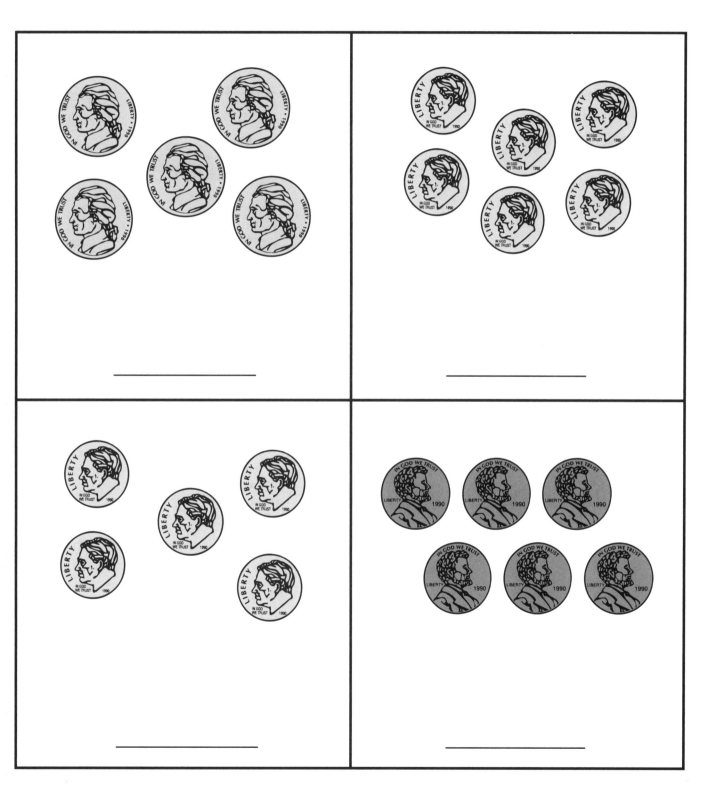

Name: _____

Circle the correct number in each box.

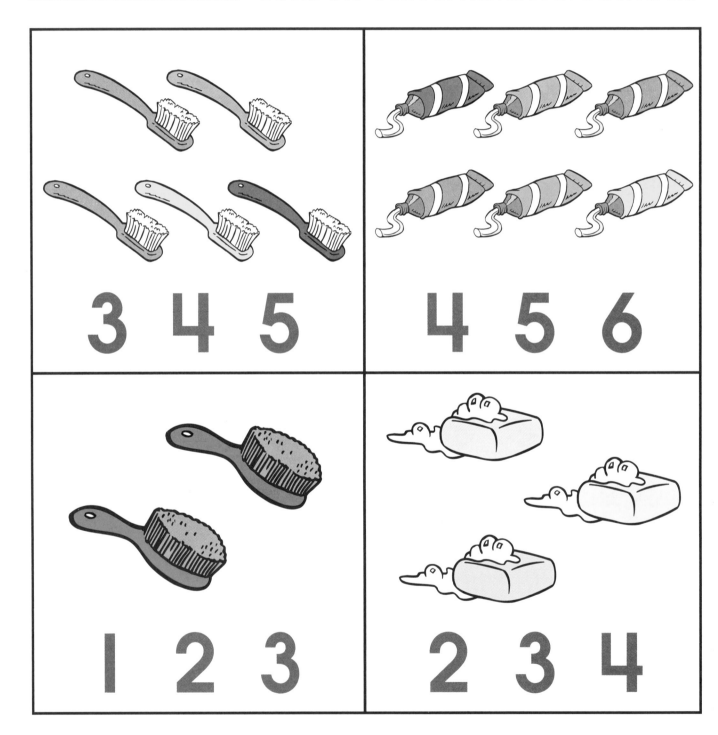

Name: _____

Look at the picture. Read the questions.
Circle the correct number.

◆ How many in all?   1   2   3

◆ How many in all?   4   5   6

◆ How many in all?   3   4   5

◆ How many in all?   4   5   6

Name: ____________________

REVIEW NUMBERS 1-6

Count each group of blocks. Trace each number. Then count each group of blocks below. Write the number.

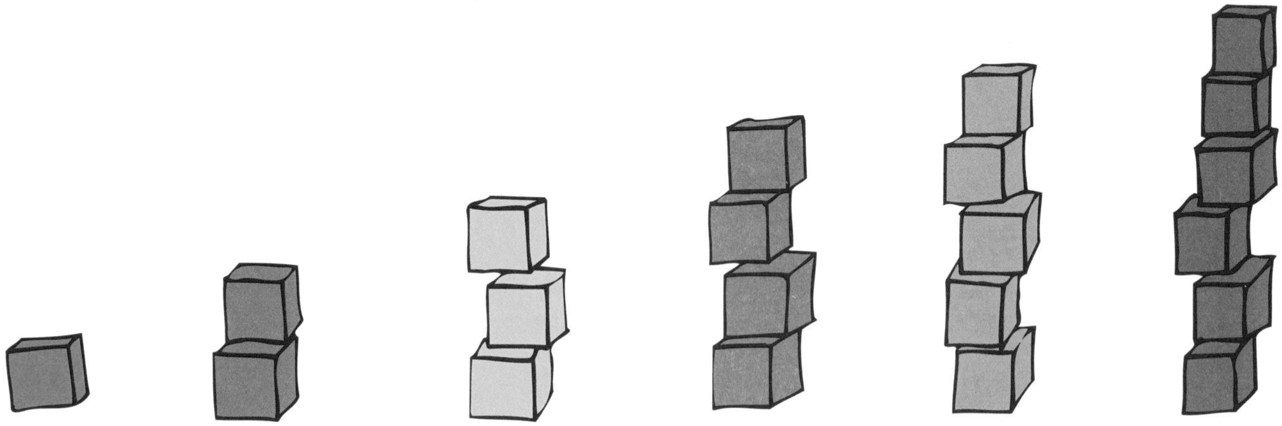

1 2 3 4 5 6

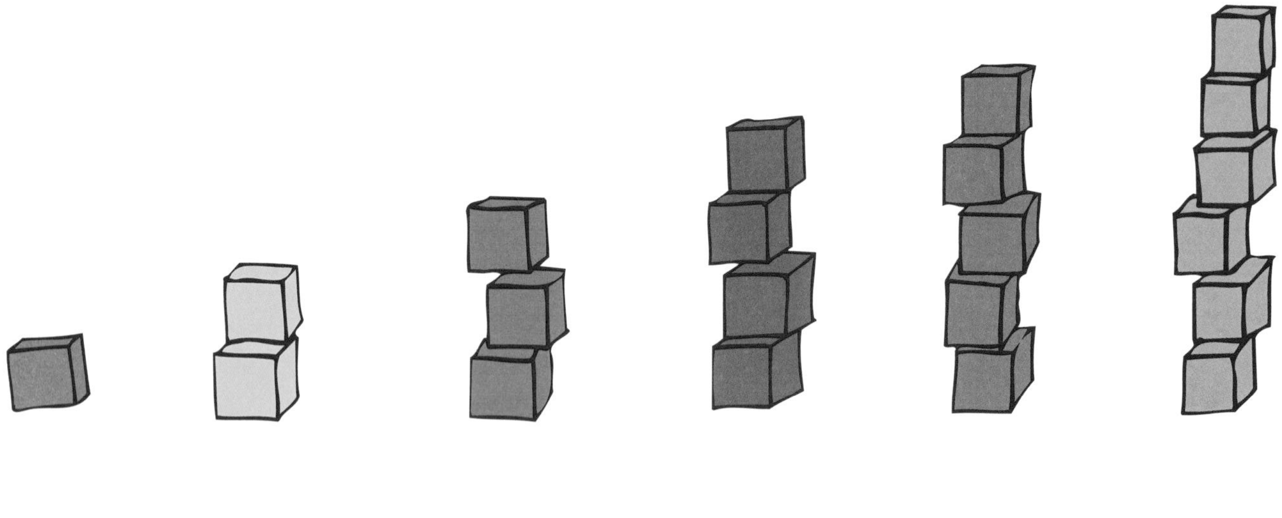

______ ______ ______ ______ ______ ______

Cut out the dominoes below and on pages 387–389. Lay down one domino. Then match another domino with the same number of dots to the first domino. Continue matching dominoes until you have used all the dominoes.

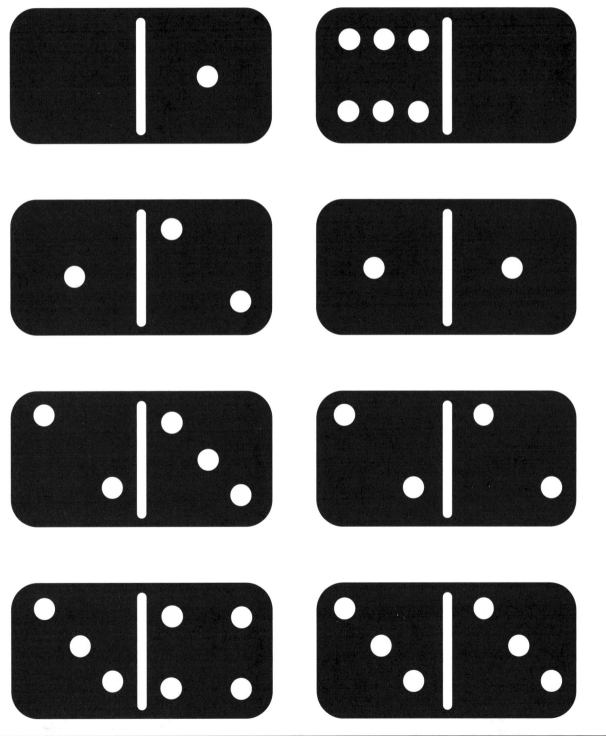

Numbers and Counting

Numbers and Counting

Trace and write the number **7**. Then draw seven cookies.

SEVEN
7

Trace and write the number word.
Count the ladybugs. Connect the dots.
Color the picture.

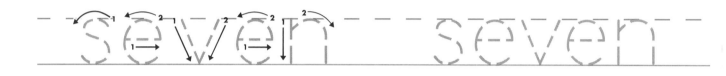

2•   •3

    1•————————•7

•4

6•   •5

EIGHT
8

Trace and write the number **8**. Then draw eight peas on the plate.

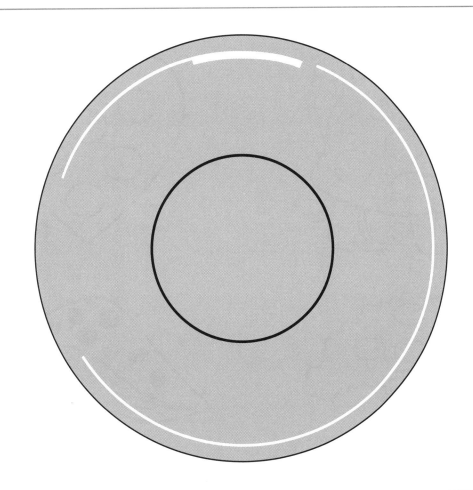

EIGHT
8

Trace and write the number word. Color the pictures that have eight spots.

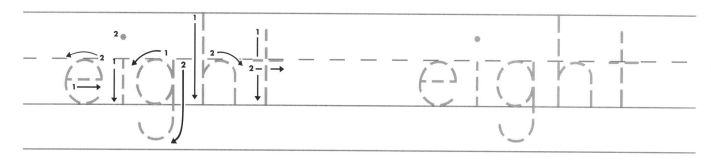

Name: _____

Count and write the number in each box. Circle the groups of seven. Color the groups of eight.

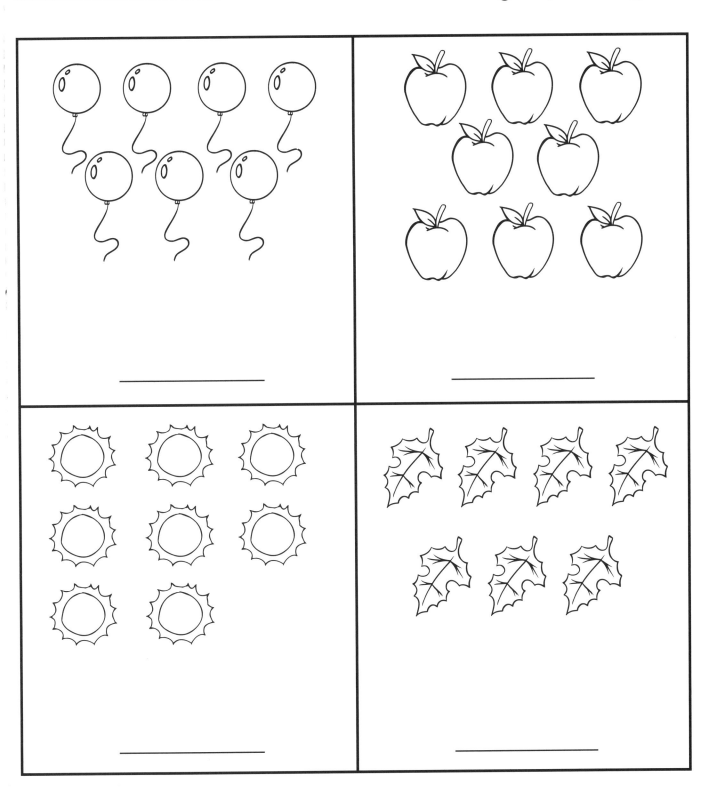

NINE AND TEN
9, 10

Trace and write the numbers **9** and **10**.
Then count and write the numbers.

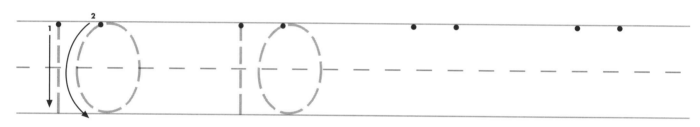

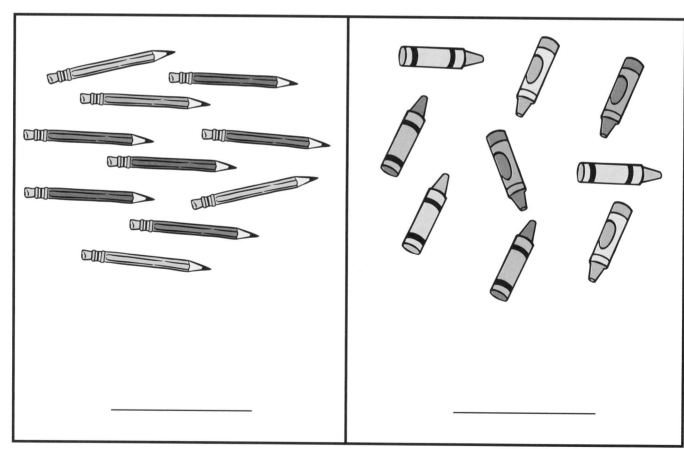

NINE

9

Trace and write the number word. Count the shapes on each quilt square below. Color the squares with nine shapes green. Color the other squares yellow.

nine   nine

TEN

10

Name:_____

Trace and write the number word.
Write the numbers 1 to 10 on the
empty hearts.

NINE AND TEN

Name: _____

Count and write the number in each box. Circle the groups of nine. Color the groups of ten.

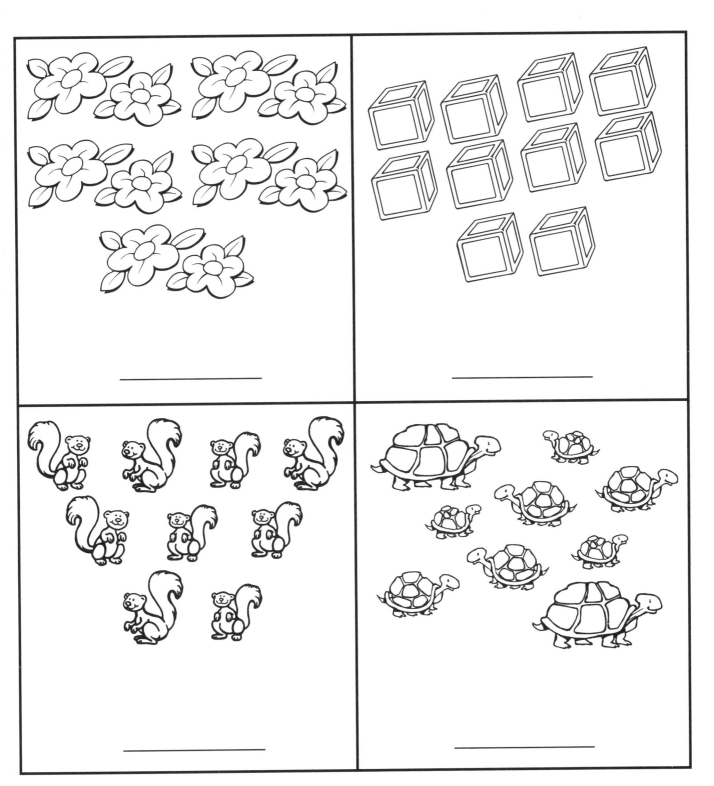

Numbers and Counting

Name: _____

Circle the correct number in each box.

7   8   9

8   9   10

REVIEW NUMBERS 7-10

Circle the correct number in each box.

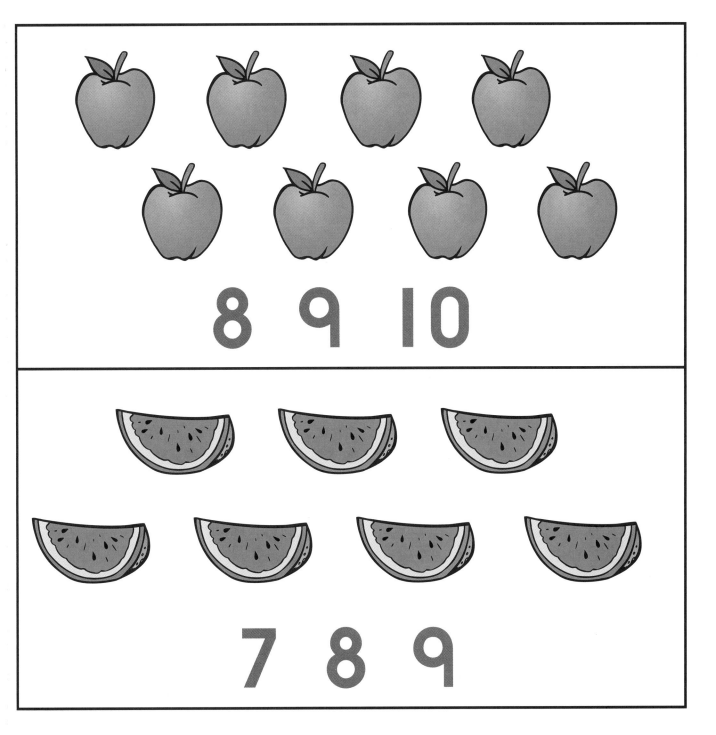

Name: _____

Count each group of balloons. Trace each number. Then count each group of balloons below. Write the number.

_____   _____   _____   _____

Name: _____

Count the beads in each group. Write the number.

_____

_____

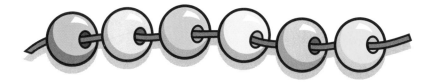

_____

_____

_____

REVIEW NUMBERS 1-10

Connect the dots from 1 to 10. Then color the picture.

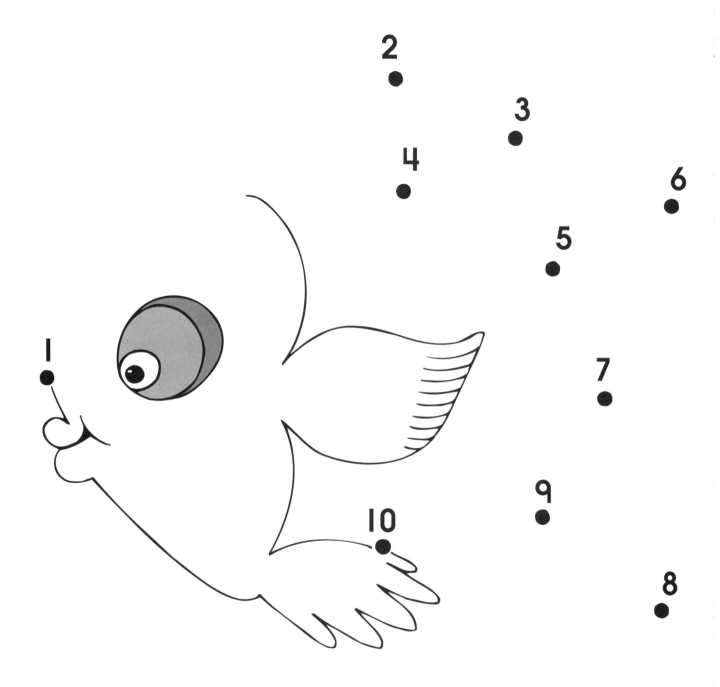

REVIEW NUMBERS 1-10

Connect the dots from 1 to 10. Then color the picture.

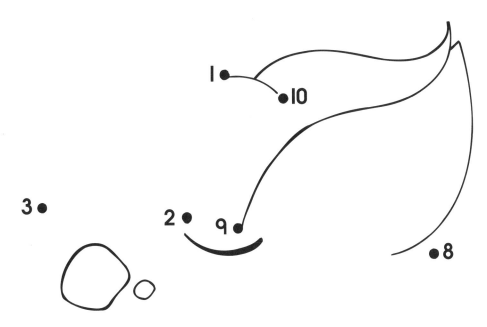

Name: _____

Count your fingers on both hands. Write the numbers.

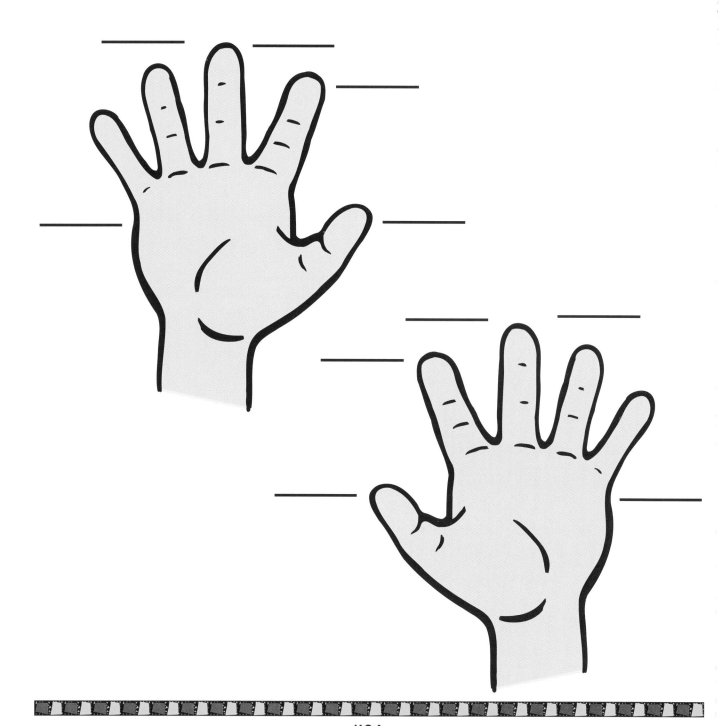

REVIEW NUMBERS 1-10

Name: _____

Count your toes on both feet. Write the numbers.

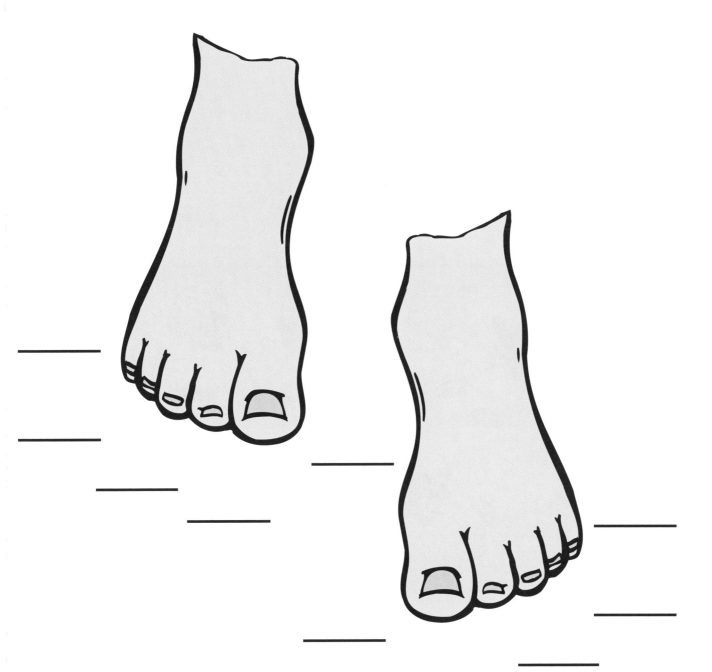

ELEVEN AND TWELVE
11, 12

Trace and write the numbers **11** and **12**.
Then count and write the numbers.

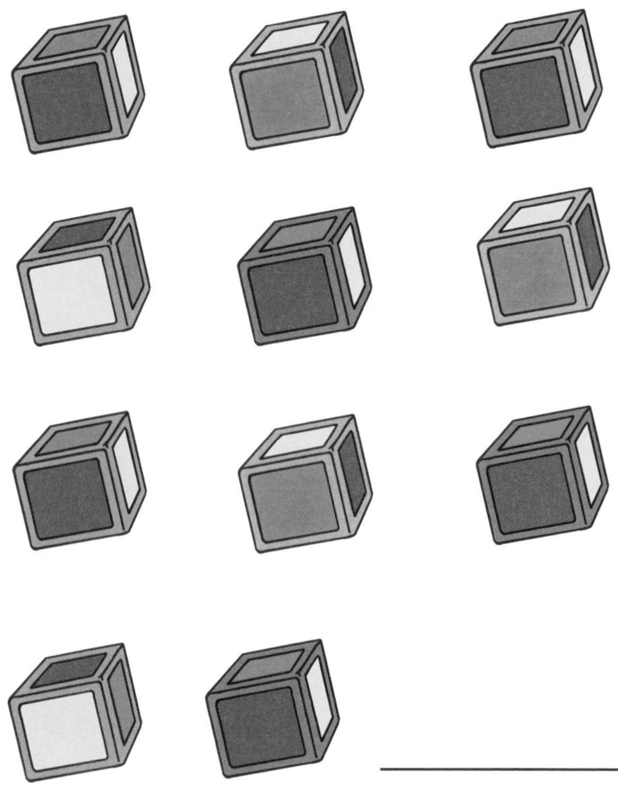

11 11 11 11 • • • •

12 12 • •

_____   _____

Name: _____

Write the number in each box. Circle the groups of eleven. Color the groups of twelve.

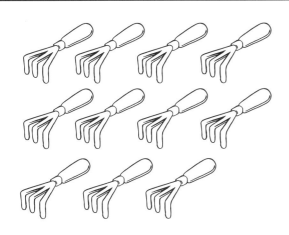

_____

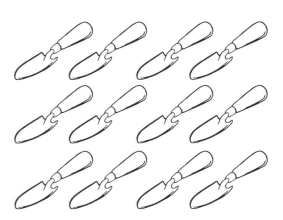

_____

_____

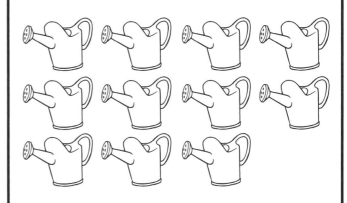

_____

Numbers and Counting

ELEVEN

11

Name: _____

Count Zeb Zebra's stripes and color them.

TWELVE
12

Name: _____

Count each group of creatures. Draw a line from the creatures to their matching apples.

Name: _____

Draw flowers to show the number in each box.

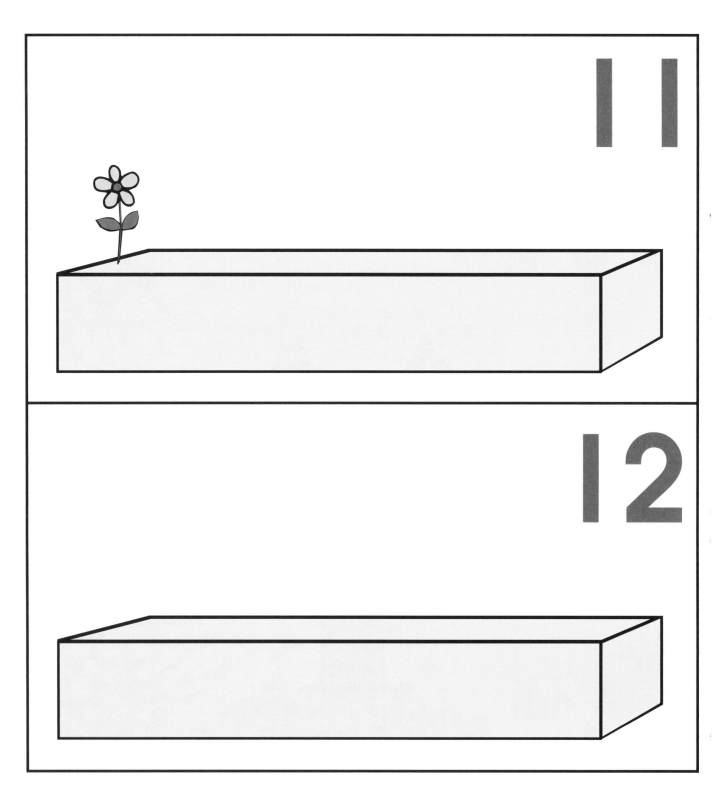

REVIEW NUMBERS 1-12

Name: _____

Count the number of colored squares.
Then write the correct number.

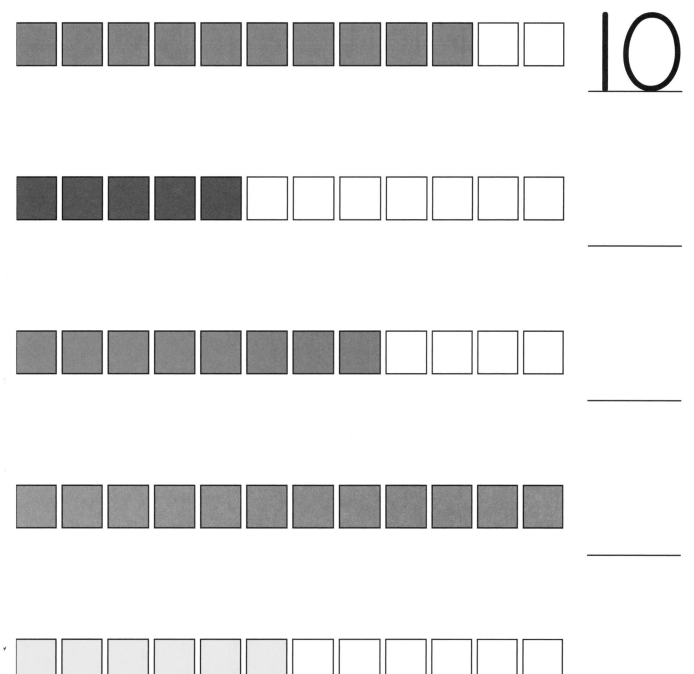

10

_____

_____

_____

_____

Numbers and Counting

REVIEW NUMBERS 1-12

Name: ______________________________

Count the number of colored squares.
Then write the correct number.

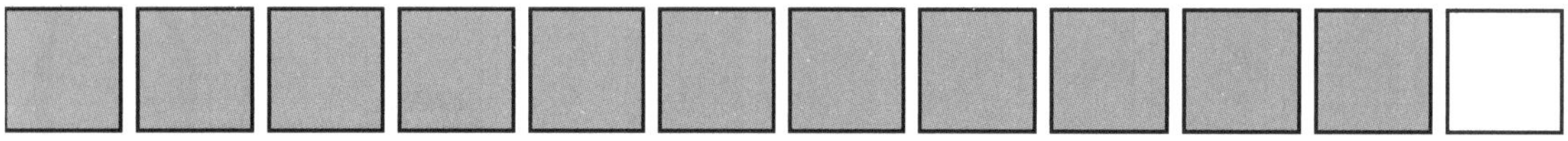

____

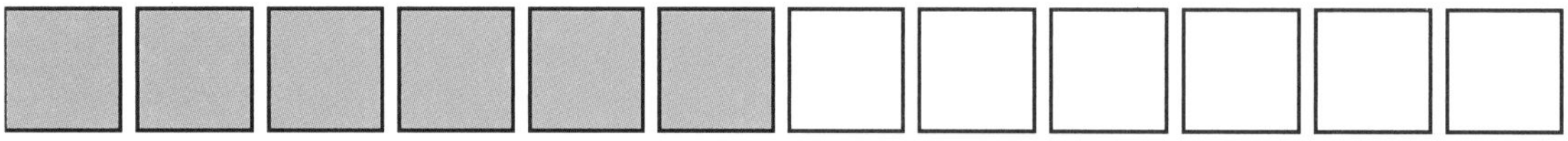

____

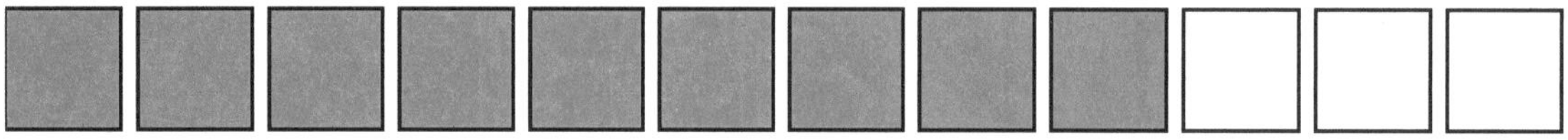

____

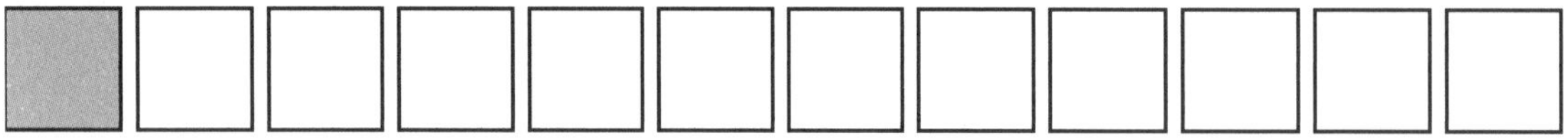

____

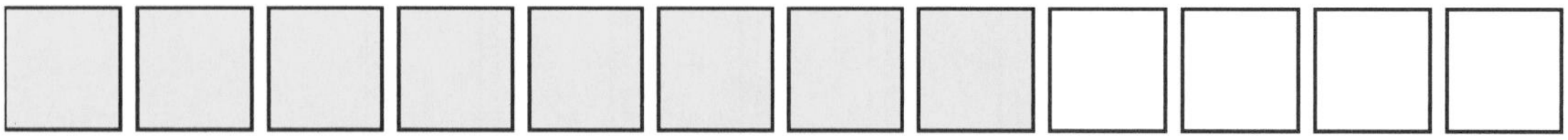

____

THIRTEEN

13

Name: _____

Trace and write the number **13**.
Complete each puzzle by writing or
drawing the missing number of flowers.

13 13

13

FOURTEEN
14

Trace and write the number 14.
Connect the dots. Color the picture.

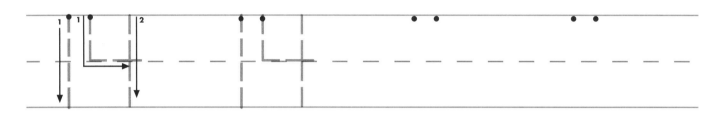

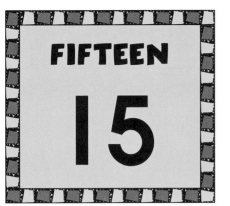

FIFTEEN

15

Trace and write the number **15**.
Write the missing pool ball numbers.

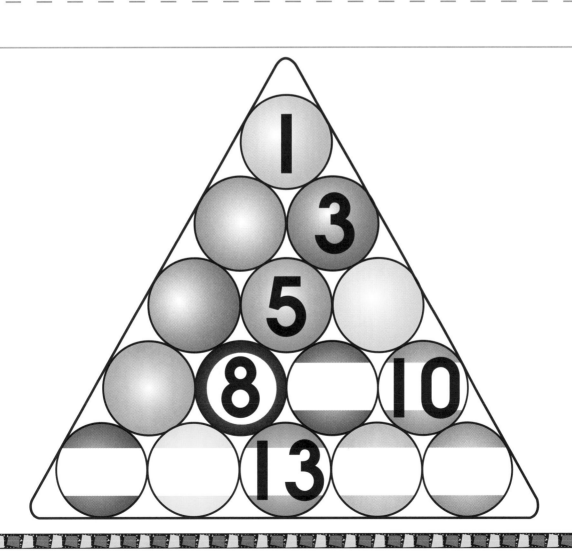

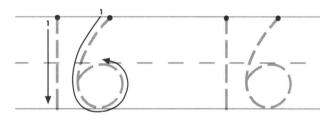

SIXTEEN

16

Name: _____

Trace and write the number **16**. Draw eight legs on each spider.

How many legs are there in all? _____

SEVENTEEN
17

Name: _____

Trace and write the number **17**. Circle each group of **17** things. Color the dog.

Numbers and Counting

EIGHTEEN
18

Trace and write the number **18**. Help Filbert Fish find his way to the top. Write the numbers 1–18 in each bubble along the way.

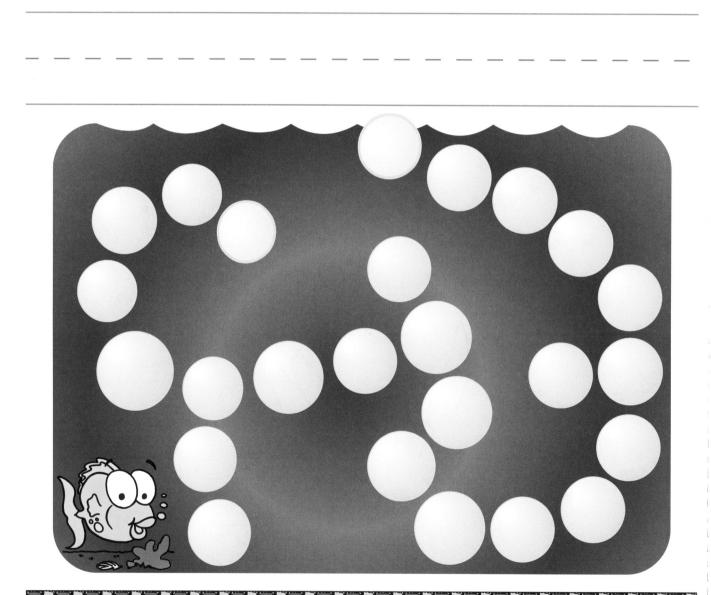

NINETEEN

19

Name: _____

Trace and write the number **19**. Circle the numbers 1–19 in the picture.

Numbers and Counting

TWENTY

20

Name: _____

Trace and write the number **20**.
Connect the dots to find the
hidden picture.

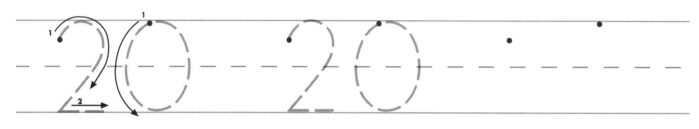

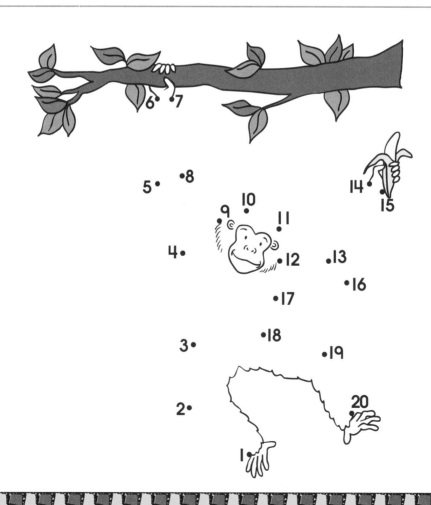

TIME AND MONEY

HOW MUCH TIME

Name: _____

Look at the pictures. Circle the picture in each row that takes more time.

TIME

Trace the numbers 1–12 in order on the clock.

Hickory Dickory Dock,
The mouse ran up the clock.
The clock struck one and down he ran.
Hickory Dickory Dock.

TIME

Write the time that is on
each clock.

Example:

__2__ **o'clock**

_____ **o'clock**

_____ **o'clock**

_____ **o'clock**

TIME

Write the time that is on each clock.

 _____ o'clock

 _____ o'clock

 _____ o'clock

 _____ o'clock

Time and Money

PENNIES

Name: _____

A penny is worth 1¢. It is brown. Circle the correct amount of money in each row below.

Example:

1¢ (2¢) 3¢

1¢ 2¢ 3¢

5¢ 6¢ 7¢

7¢ 8¢ 9¢

PENNIES

Circle the correct amount of money in each row below.

      2¢ 3¢ 4¢

     1¢ 2¢ 3¢

       4¢ 5¢ 6¢

   **7¢ 8¢ 9¢**

Time and Money

NICKELS

Name: _____

A nickel is worth 5¢. It is silver. Circle the correct amount of money in each row below.

Example:

 =

5¢   **5¢**

4¢ 5¢ 6¢

1¢ 2¢ 3¢

1¢ 2¢ 3¢

NICKELS

Name: _____

Circle the correct amount of money in each row below.

      3¢   4¢   5¢

   4¢   5¢   6¢

     3¢   4¢   5¢

    4¢   5¢   6¢

Time and Money

DIMES

Name: _____

A dime is worth 10¢. It is silver.
Circle the correct amount of
money in each row below.

Example:

10¢   10¢   10¢

          1¢ 5¢ 10¢

5¢ 7¢ 10¢

          8¢ 9¢ 10¢

DIMES

Circle the correct amount of money in each row below.

  2¢   3¢   4¢

   5¢   6¢   7¢

   8¢   9¢   10¢

   9¢   10¢   11¢

Name: _____

PENNY, NICKEL, DIME

Color each penny brown. Draw a line under each nickel. Draw a circle around each dime.

 penny

nickel

dime

Name: _____

Match the price of the thing to the correct amount of money.

Time and Money

Name: _____

Match the coins to the correct amount of money.

         |0¢

         5¢

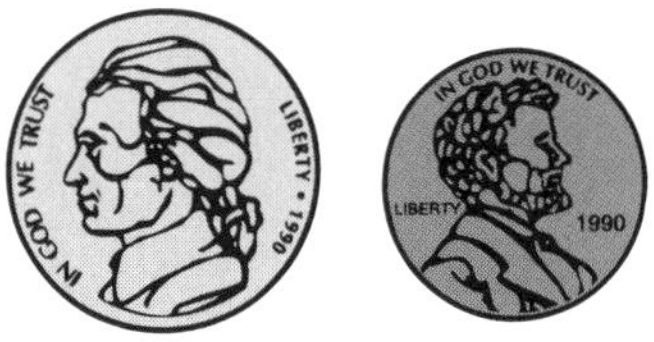

        2¢

        6¢

 |¢

   8¢

PATTERNS, GRAPHING AND THINKING SKILLS

SHAPE PATTERNS

Circle the shape that comes next in each pattern.

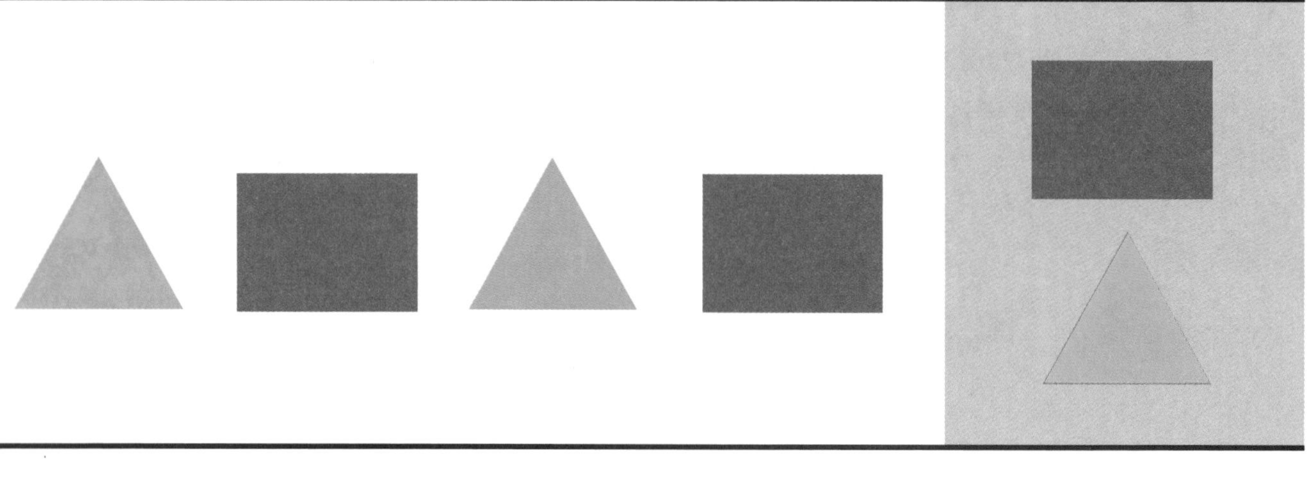

Name: _____

Draw and color the shape that comes next in each pattern.

Patterns, Graphing and Thinking Skills

SHAPE PATTERNS

Name: _____

Draw and color the shape that comes next in each pattern.

SHAPE PATTERNS

Name:_____

Draw and color the shape that comes next in each pattern.

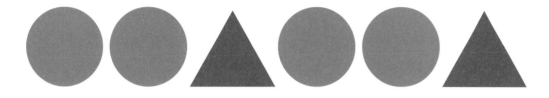

Patterns, Graphing and Thinking Skills

SHAPE PATTERNS

Name: _____

Draw the shape that comes next in the pattern.

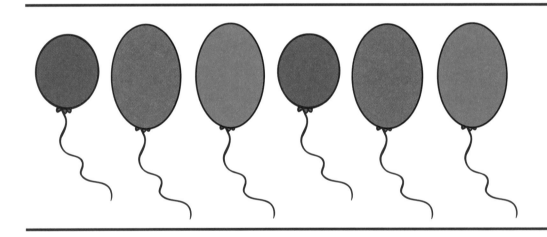

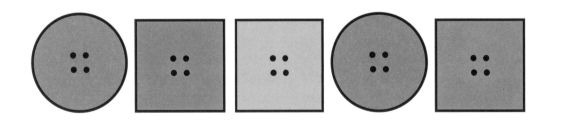

Name: _____

Count the pets in the window.
Then color one box for each
animal on the graph below.

6				
5				
4				
3				
2				
1				

GRAPHING

Name: _____

Count the shapes in the picture.
Then complete the graph below.

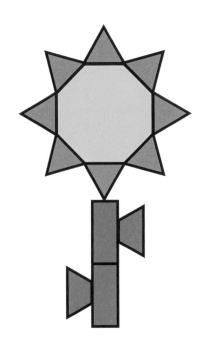

8			
7			
6			
5			
4			
3			
2			
1			

◀ ▲ ▬ ⬡

GRAPHING

Name:_____

Look at the graph on page 444.
Then answer the questions below.

◆ How many triangles are there? _____

◆ How many rectangles are there? _____

◆ How many octogons are there? _____

◆ How many trapezoids are there? _____

◆ Which two shapes are there the same number of?

_____ and _____

◆ How many shapes are there all together?_____

Patterns, Graphing and Thinking Skills

GRAPHING

Name: _____

Look at the graph below. Then answer the questions on page 447.

10			
9			
8			
7			
6			
5			
4			
3			
2			
1			

hot dog   hamburger   pizza   chicken

GRAPHING

Name: _____

Answer the questions about the graph on page 446.

◆ How many people like hot dogs best? _____

◆ How many people like pizza best? _____

◆ How many people like chicken best? _____

◆ Which food do most people like best? _____

◆ Which two foods do the same number of people like best?

_____and _____

◆ Which food do the fewest number of people like best?

_____

THINKING SKILLS

Read the clues below. Draw an **X** on the umbrellas that do not fit the clues. Circle the correct umbrella.

◆ The umbrella is open.
◆ The umbrella is big.
◆ The umbrella has dots on it.

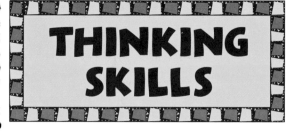

THINKING SKILLS

Name: _____

Read the clues below. Draw an **X** on the bicycles that do not fit the clues. Circle the correct bicycle.

◆ The bicycle has a bell.
◆ The bicycle is blue.
◆ The bicycle has a flat tire.

Patterns, Graphing and Thinking Skills

THINKING SKILLS

Name: _____

Read the clues below. Draw an **X** on the houses that do not fit the clues. Circle the correct house.

◆ The house is white.
◆ The house has a red door.
◆ The house has a fence in front of it.

THINKING SKILLS

Name: _____

Read the clues below. Draw an **X** on the mittens that do not fit the clues. Circle the correct mitten.

◆ The mitten is green.
◆ The mitten has 2 different shapes on it.
◆ The mitten has hearts on it.

451

Patterns, Graphing and Thinking Skills

Name: _____

Read the clues below. Draw an **X** on the numbers that do not fit the clues. Circle the correct number.

◆ The number is greater than 1.
◆ The number is less than 6.
◆ The number is not 2.

7

5

2

0

Read the clues below. Draw an **X** on the numbers that do not fit the clues. Circle the correct number.

◆ The number is less than 7.
◆ The number is greater than 2.
◆ The number equals 3 + 1.

8

3

4

1

APPENDIX

THE MANUSCRIPT ALPHABET
SHAPES, COLORS AND NUMBERS
BIBLIOGRAPHY
GLOSSARY
ANSWER KEY
TEACHING SUGGESTIONS

THE MANUSCRIPT ALPHABET

SHAPES, COLORS AND NUMBERS

circle

square

rectangle

triangle

red

yellow

orange

purple

blue

green

black

brown

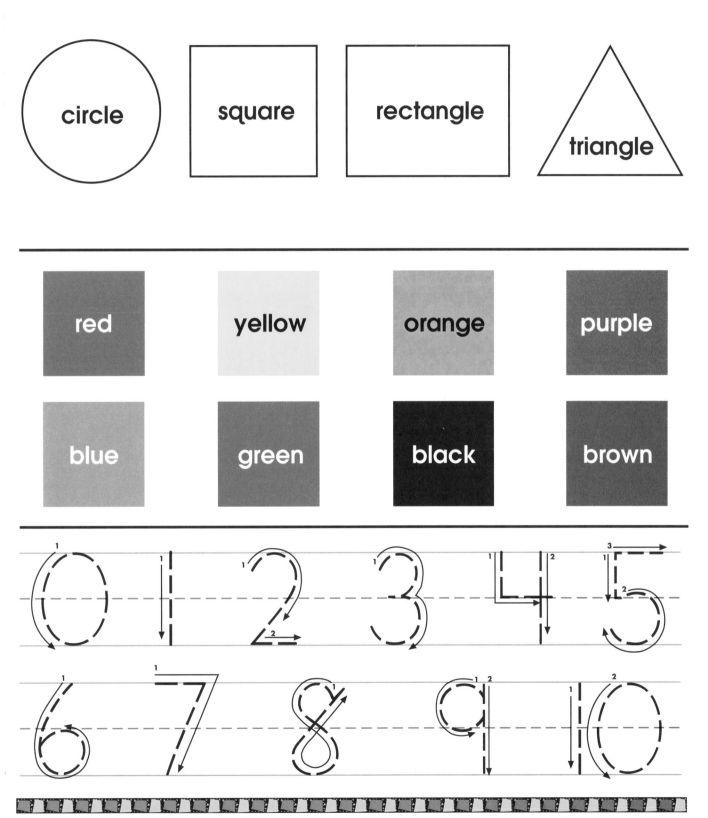

BIBLIOGRAPHY

- **Animal Orchestra: A Counting Book** by Scott Gustafson

- **Anno's Counting Book** by Mitsumasa Anno

- **Are You My Mother?** by P. D. Eastman

- **Boomer Goes to School** by Constance McGeorge

- **Count-A-Saurus** by Nancy Blumenthal

- **Curious George** by H. A. Rey

- **Count and See** by Tana Hoban

- **Elmer** by David McKee

- **A Fishy Color Story** by Joanne and David Wylie

- **A Fishy Shape Story** by Joanne and David Wylie

- **Franklin Plays the Game** by Paulette Bourgeois

- **The Giving Tree** by Shel Silverstein

- **Have You Seen My Cat?** by Eric Carle

- **I Know About Counting** by Henry Pluckrose

- **How Many Bugs in a Box?** by David Carter

- **I Love Colors** by Stan and Jan Berenstain

- **Just Like Daddy** by Frank Asch

- **The Little Red Hen** by Paul Galdone

BIBLIOGRAPHY

- **Peter Rabbit's 1 2 3** by Beatrix Potter

- **My Many Colored Days** by Dr. Seuss

- **Animal Babies 1 2 3** by Eve Spencer

- **The Napping House** by Audrey Wood

- **Numbers** by Monique Felix

- **Numbers at Play: A Counting Book** by Charles Sullivan

- **Pumpkin, Pumpkin** by Jeanne Titherington

- **Q Is for Duck** by Mary Elting and Michael Folsom

- **Rainbow Fish** by Marcus Pfister

- **Somebody and the Three Blairs** by Marilyn Tolhurst

- **Ten Apples up on top** by Theo LeSeig

- **Ten Bears in a Bed** by John Richardson

- **The Three Bears** by Byron Barton

- **The Very Busy Spider** by Eric Carle

- **The Very Hungry Caterpillar** by Eric Carle

- **The Wheels on the Bus** by Harriet Ziefert

- **Where's My Teddy?** by Jez Alborough

- **White Rabbit's Color Book** by Alan Baker

GLOSSARY

- **ABC Order:** Putting letters or words in the order in which they appear in the alphabet.

- **Beginning Consonant:** The sound made by the first letter of a word or a picture name.

- **Capital Letters:** Letters that are used at the beginning of names of people and places. They are also used at the beginning of sentences.

- **Consonants:** The letters of the alphabet excluding the five vowels a, e, i, o and u. The consonants are b, c, d, f, g, h, j, k, l, m, n, p, q, r, s, t, v, w, x, y and z.

- **Ending Consonant:** The sound made by the last letter of a word or a picture name.

- **Graphing:** Using a diagram to show the relationship between two or more sets of objects with pictures.

- **Lowercase letters:** The letters which are often called "small" letters. They are the letters a, b, c, d, e, f, g, h, i, j, k, l, m, n, o, p, q, r, s, t, u, v, w, x, y and z.

- **Measuring:** The process of determining the size, quantity or amount of something.

- **Opposites:** Things that are different in every way.

GLOSSARY

- **Ordinal Numbers:** Numbers that show order in a series, such as first, second or third.

- **Patterns:** Recognizing a series of shapes or designs that are similar to a given one.

- **Rhyme:** Words with the same ending sound.

- **Riddles:** Questions in which clues to an answer are provided.

- **Sequencing:** Putting things in logical order.

- **Short Vowels:** The letters a, e, i, o and u. Short vowel a is the sound heard in cat; short vowel e is the sound heard in hen; short vowel i is the sound heard in pig; short vowel o is the sound heard in fox; short vowel u is the sound heard in tub.

- **Thinking Skills:** Problem solving skills, such as deductive reasoning, classifying, making inferences, comparing, brainstorming, etc. that enable people to think creatively and logically.

- **Uppercase letters:** The letters of the alphabet which are called "capital" letters. They are A, B, C, D, E, F, G, H, I, J, K, L, M, N, O, P, Q, R, S, T, U, V, W, X, Y and Z.

- **Word Recognition:** The ability to read or recognize words.

ANSWER KEY

RED Color each picture red. Then draw a picture of something else red.

Answers will vary.

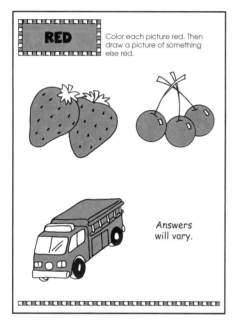

10

YELLOW Color each picture yellow. Then draw a picture of something else yellow.

Answers will vary.

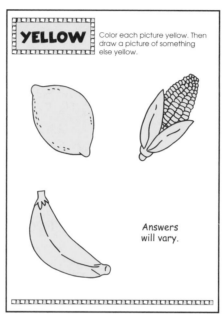

11

BLUE Circle the blue picture in each row.

12

GREEN Color each picture green. Then draw a picture of something else green.

Answers will vary.

13

ORANGE Circle the orange picture in each row.

14

PURPLE Color each picture purple. Then draw a picture of something else purple.

Answers will vary.

15

ANSWER KEY

BLACK Circle the black picture in each row.

16

BROWN Circle the brown picture in each row.

17

REVIEW COLORS Color each picture the same color as the crayon above it.

18

REVIEW COLORS Color the picture.

Results will vary.

19

REVIEW COLORS Color the fruits and vegetables.

Results will vary.

20

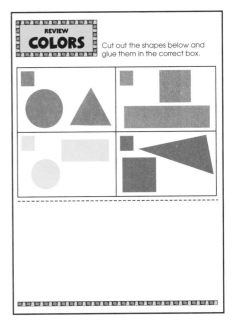

REVIEW COLORS Cut out the shapes below and glue them in the correct box.

21

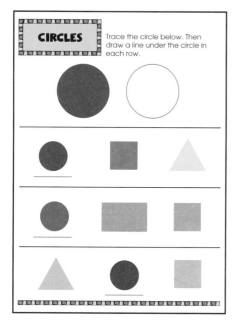

CIRCLES — Trace the circle below. Then draw a line under the circle in each row.

23

CIRCLES — Circles can be different sizes. Trace the circles below. Then color the pictures.

Results will vary.

24

CIRCLES — Draw an X on the pictures that have the shape of a circle.

25

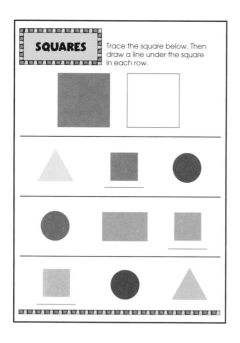

SQUARES — Trace the square below. Then draw a line under the square in each row.

26

SQUARES — Squares have 4 sides of the same length. Help Sue get home. Color the path that has only squares.

Sue

Home

27

SQUARES — Draw an X on the pictures that have the shape of a square.

28

ANSWER KEY

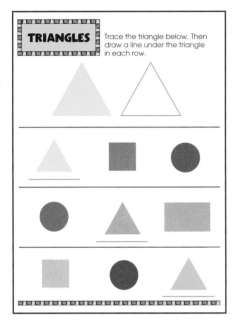

TRIANGLES Trace the triangle below. Then draw a line under the triangle in each row.

29

TRIANGLES All triangles have 3 sides. Triangles can be different sizes. Trace and color the triangle shapes below.

30

TRIANGLES Draw an **X** on the pictures that have the shape of a triangle.

31

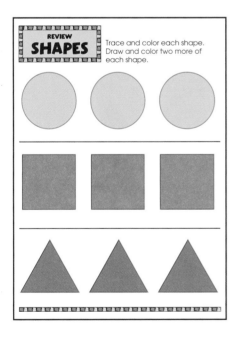

REVIEW SHAPES Trace and color each shape. Draw and color two more of each shape.

32

REVIEW SHAPES AND COLORS Look at the shapes in the picture.

◆ Color the circles blue.
◆ Color the squares red.
◆ Color the triangles green.

33

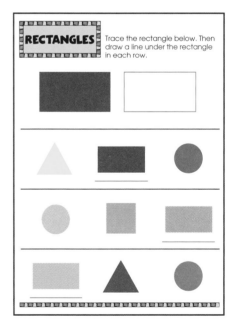

RECTANGLES Trace the rectangle below. Then draw a line under the rectangle in each row.

34

ANSWER KEY

RECTANGLES All rectangles have 4 sides, but only the opposite sides are the same length.

Look at the shapes. Color the rectangles.

Draw a circle around each picture that has the shape of a rectangle.

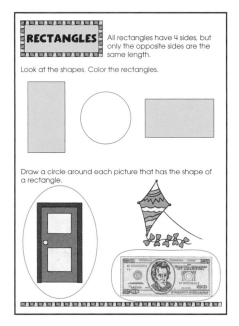

35

RECTANGLES Draw an **X** on the pictures that have the shape of a rectangle.

36

REVIEW SHAPES Name the shape at the beginning of each row. Circle the shape in that row that is the same.

circle   rectangle   triangle

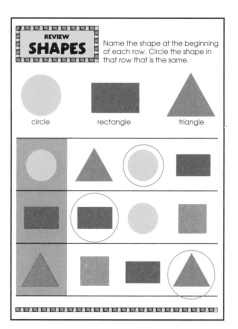

37

REVIEW SHAPES

Draw a box around the circle.

Draw a box around the square.

Draw a box around the triangle.

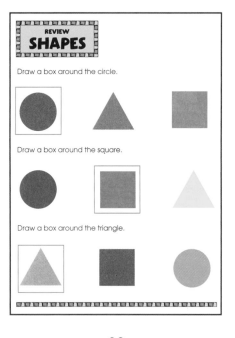

38

REVIEW SHAPES Look at the picture.

◆ Color the circle.
◆ Draw a line from the rectangle to the hippo.
◆ Draw an **X** on the squares.
◆ Circle the triangle.

39

REVIEW SHAPES Color the shapes to complete this picture.

◆ Color the squares yellow.
◆ Color the triangles red.
◆ Color the rectangles green.

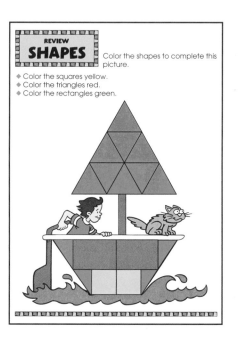

40

ANSWER KEY

SHAPE ART Cut out the shapes and glue them on paper to make a picture.

Results will vary.

41

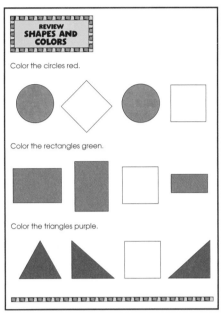

REVIEW SHAPES AND COLORS

Color the circles red.

Color the rectangles green.

Color the triangles purple.

43

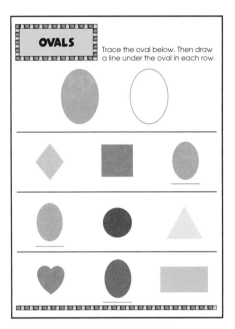

OVALS Trace the oval below. Then draw a line under the oval in each row.

44

OVALS Ovals can be different sizes. Color the oval shapes below.

45

OVALS Draw an **X** on the pictures that have the shape of an oval.

46

DIAMONDS Trace the diamond below. Then draw a line under the diamond in each row.

47

ANSWER KEY

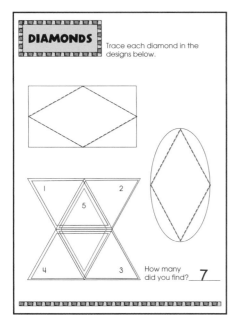

DIAMONDS Trace each diamond in the designs below.

How many did you find? __7__

48

DIAMONDS Help Jim get to the kite shop. Color the path that has only diamonds.

Jim

Kite Shop

49

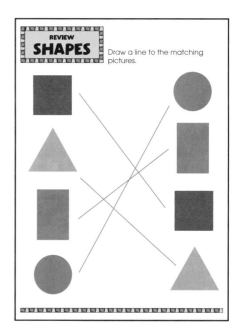

REVIEW SHAPES Draw a line to the matching pictures.

50

STARS Trace the star below. Then draw a line under the star in each row.

51

STARS Stars can be different sizes. Color the star shapes below.

52

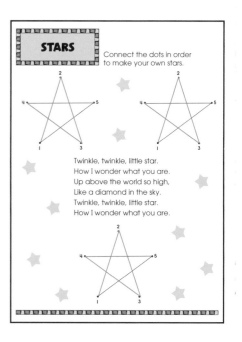

STARS Connect the dots in order to make your own stars.

Twinkle, twinkle, little star.
How I wonder what you are.
Up above the world so high,
Like a diamond in the sky.
Twinkle, twinkle, little star.
How I wonder what you are.

53

ANSWER KEY

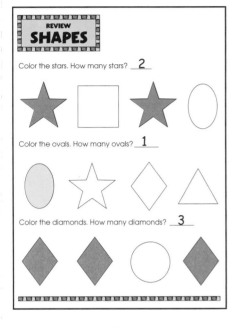

REVIEW SHAPES

Color the stars. How many stars? __2__

Color the ovals. How many ovals? __1__

Color the diamonds. How many diamonds? __3__

54

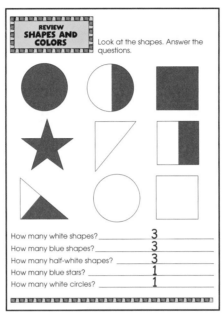

REVIEW SHAPES AND COLORS

Look at the shapes. Answer the questions.

How many white shapes? __3__
How many blue shapes? __3__
How many half-white shapes? __3__
How many blue stars? __1__
How many white circles? __1__

55

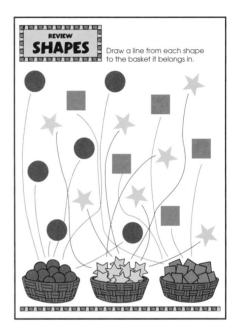

REVIEW SHAPES

Draw a line from each shape to the basket it belongs in.

56

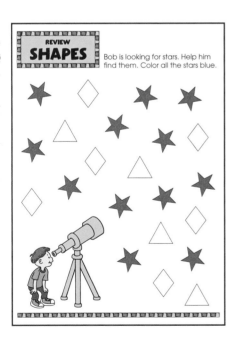

REVIEW SHAPES

Bob is looking for stars. Help him find them. Color all the stars blue.

57

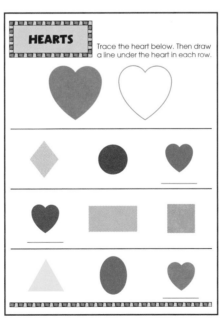

HEARTS

Trace the heart below. Then draw a line under the heart in each row.

58

HEARTS

Hearts can be different sizes. Color the heart shapes below.

59

ANSWER KEY

HEARTS Draw an **X** on the hearts in the picture below.

60

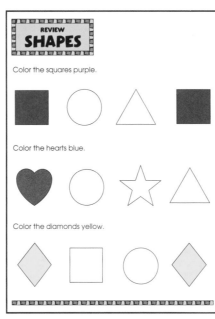

REVIEW SHAPES

Color the squares purple.

Color the hearts blue.

Color the diamonds yellow.

61

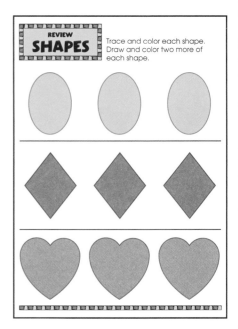

REVIEW SHAPES Trace and color each shape. Draw and color two more of each shape.

62

SHAPE RIDDLE Read the riddle. Write and draw the answer.

I am a food.
I am cold.
I have a triangle under me.
What am I?

ice cream

63

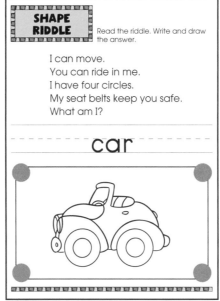

SHAPE RIDDLE Read the riddle. Write and draw the answer.

I can move.
You can ride in me.
I have four circles.
My seat belts keep you safe.
What am I?

car

64

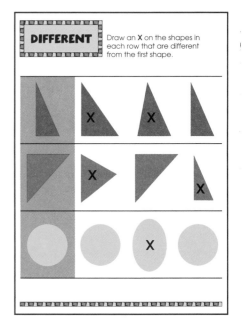

DIFFERENT Draw an **X** on the shapes in each row that are different from the first shape.

65

ANSWER KEY

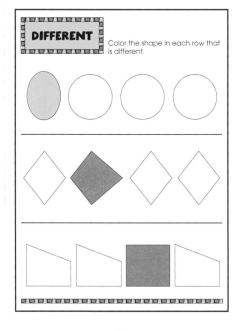

DIFFERENT Color the shape in each row that is different.

66

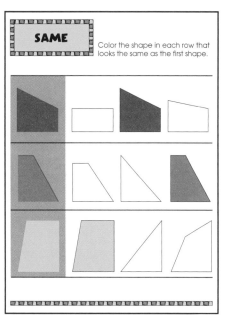

SAME Color the shape in each row that looks the same as the first shape.

67

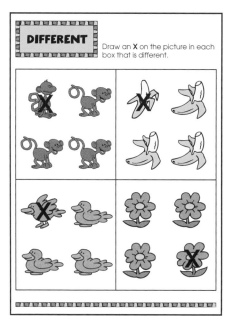

DIFFERENT Draw an **X** on the picture in each box that is different.

68

THINGS THAT GO TOGETHER Color the pictures in each row that go together. Draw an **X** on the one that does not belong.

69

THINGS THAT GO TOGETHER Color the pictures in each row that go together. Draw an **X** on the one that does not belong.

70

THINGS THAT GO TOGETHER Draw an **X** on the picture that does not belong. Draw another thing that does belong.

Answers will vary.

71

ANSWER KEY

THINGS THAT GO TOGETHER — Draw an **X** on the picture that does not belong. Draw another thing that does belong.

Answers will vary.

72

THINGS THAT GO TOGETHER — Cut out the boxes below and on page 75. Match the pictures that go together.

73

THINGS THAT GO TOGETHER

75

OPPOSITES — **Opposites** are things that are different in every way. Draw a line to match the opposites.

day
front
happy
big
little
sad
night
back

77

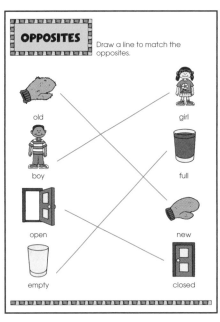

OPPOSITES — Draw a line to match the opposites.

old
boy
open
empty
girl
full
new
closed

78

OPPOSITES — Draw a picture of the opposite.

day	Night picture
	night
sad	Happy face
	happy

79

ANSWER KEY

OPPOSITES
Draw a picture of the opposite.

wet | Dry boy
dry
Rabbit going under the fence
over | under

80

BIG
Look at the pictures in each box. Circle the pictures that are big.

81

SMALL
Look at the pictures in each box. Circle the pictures that are small.

82

BIG AND SMALL
Color the small pictures in each box orange. Color the big pictures purple.

83

BIG AND SMALL
Color the small pictures in each box green. Color the big pictures yellow.

84

SMALLEST TO BIGGEST
Cut out the boxes below. Put the animals in order from smallest to biggest.

85

ANSWER KEY

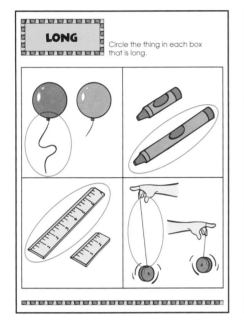

87

88

89

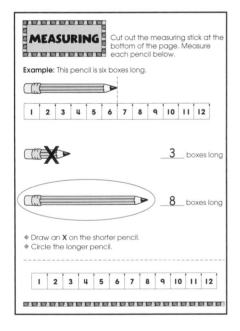

90

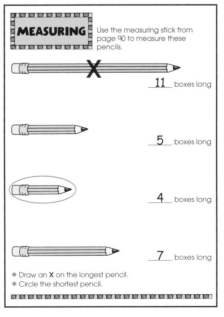

91

92

ANSWER KEY

TALL

Circle the picture in each box that is tall.

93

TALLER AND SHORTER

Circle the picture that is taller. Draw an **X** on the picture that is shorter.

94

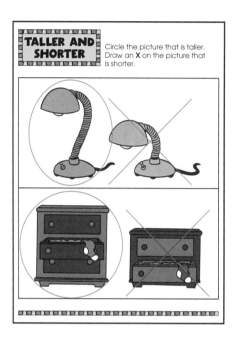

TALLER AND SHORTER

Circle the picture that is taller. Draw an **X** on the picture that is shorter.

95

FULL AND EMPTY

Circle the full container. Draw an **X** on the empty container.

96

FULL AND EMPTY

Circle the full container. Draw an **X** on the empty container.

97

ABOVE

Look at the picture. The sun is above the bird. Circle the pictures above the bird.

98

ANSWER KEY

BELOW — Look at the picture. The car is below the bird. Draw an **X** on the pictures below the bird.

99

ABOVE AND BELOW — Circle the picture that is above the others. Draw an **X** on the picture that is below the others.

100

ABOVE AND BELOW — Color the pictures above the clouds first. Then color the pictures below the clouds.

101

BETWEEN — Trace and color the cat that is between the other cats.

Color the mouse that is between the other mice.

102

BETWEEN — Color each shape that is between the other shapes.

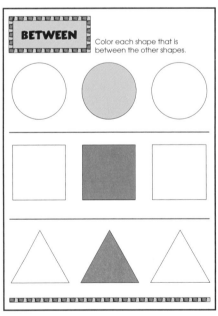

103

TOP TO BOTTOM — Draw a line from the top picture to the bottom picture.

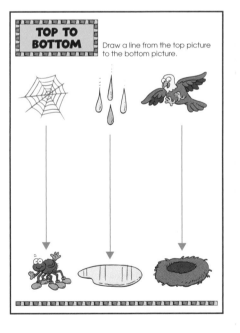

104

ANSWER KEY

TOP TO BOTTOM
Draw a line from the top picture to the bottom picture.

105

LEFT AND RIGHT
Color the pictures on the left blue. Color the pictures on the right red.

106

LEFT AND RIGHT
Color the pictures on the left green. Color the pictures on the right orange.

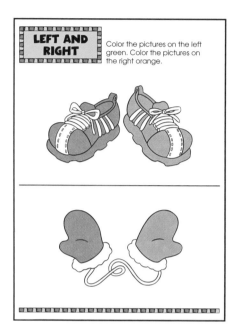

107

LEFT TO RIGHT
Draw a line from the picture on the left to the picture on the right.

108

LEFT TO RIGHT
Draw a line from the picture on the left to the picture on the right.

109

CAPITAL LETTERS
Names are special. We use **capital letters** to set them apart from other words.

Circle the capital letters in the names below.

Jacob   Mary

Erik   Emily

Lisa   Tom

Ann   Fred

Now, write your name. Circle the capital letter.

Answers will vary.

110

ANSWER KEY

WRITING YOUR NAME

Write your name. Draw a picture of yourself doing something you like.

Answers will vary.

111

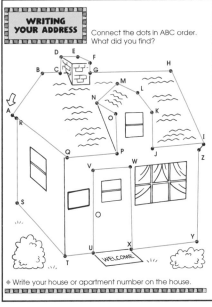

WRITING YOUR ADDRESS

Connect the dots in ABC order. What did you find?

◆ Write your house or apartment number on the house.

112

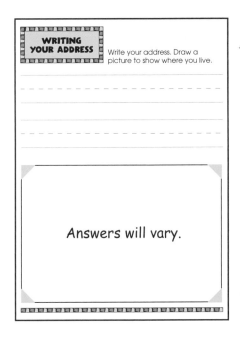

WRITING YOUR ADDRESS

Write your address. Draw a picture to show where you live.

Answers will vary.

113

WRITING YOUR PHONE NUMBER

Write your phone number. Practice dialing it using the phone below.

Answers will vary.

◆ Color the numbers in your phone number on the phone above.

114

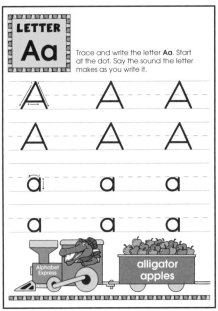

LETTER Aa

Trace and write the letter **Aa**. Start at the dot. Say the sound the letter makes as you write it.

alligator apples

116

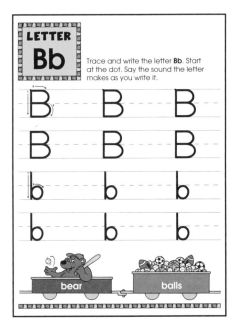

LETTER Bb

Trace and write the letter **Bb**. Start at the dot. Say the sound the letter makes as you write it.

bear   balls

117

ANSWER KEY

LETTER
Cc

Trace and write the letter **Cc**. Start at the dot. Say the sound the letter makes as you write it.

C C C
C C C
C C C
C C C

cats   cookies

118

LETTER RECOGNITION
Aa, Bb, Cc

Circle the letters in each row that match the first letter.

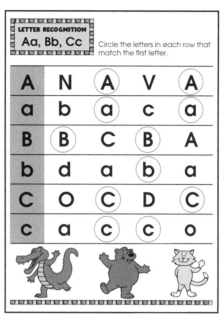

A	N	**(A)**	V	**(A)**
a	b	**(a)**	c	**(a)**
B	**(B)**	C	**(B)**	A
b	d	a	**(b)**	a
C	O	**(C)**	D	**(C)**
c	a	**(c)**	**(c)**	o

119

REVIEW
Aa, Bb, Cc

Look at the letter each insect is holding. Circle the same letter below.

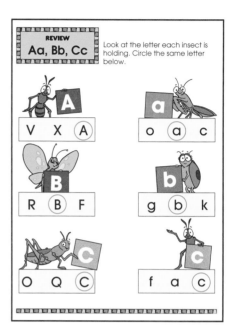

A
V X **(A)**

a
o **(a)** c

B
R **(B)** F

b
g **(b)** k

C
O Q **(C)**

c
f a **(c)**

120

LETTER
Dd

Trace and write the letter **Dd**. Start at the dot. Say the sound the letter makes as you write it.

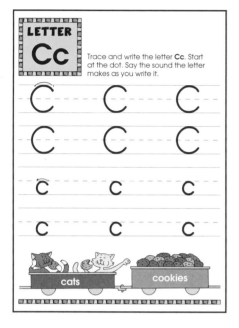

D D D
D D D
d d d
d d d

duck   dog

121

LETTER
Ee

Trace and write the letter **Ee**. Start at the dot. Say the sound the letter makes as you write it.

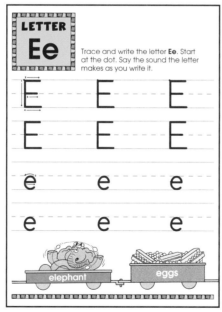

E E E
E E E
e e e
e e e

elephant   eggs

122

LETTER
Ff

Trace and write the letter **Ff**. Start at the dot. Say the sound the letter makes as you write it.

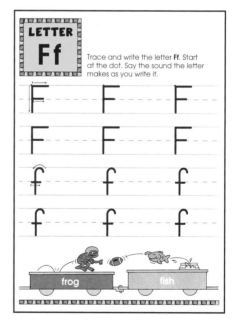

F F F
F F F
f f f
f f f

frog   fish

123

ANSWER KEY

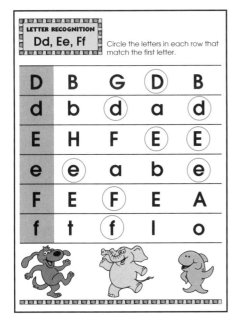

LETTER RECOGNITION
Dd, Ee, Ff

Circle the letters in each row that match the first letter.

D	B	G	(D)	B
d	b	(d)	a	(d)
E	H	F	(E)	(E)
e	(e)	a	b	(e)
F	E	(F)	E	A
f	t	(f)	l	o

124

REVIEW
Dd, Ee, Ff

Look at the uppercase letter in each row. Color each picture with a matching lowercase letter.

D	(p) (d) (b)
E	(e) (o) (e)
F	(f) (t) (l)

125

LETTER
Gg

Trace and write the letter **Gg**. Start at the dot. Say the sound the letter makes as you write it.

G G G
G G G
g g g
g g g

gorilla   goat

126

LETTER
Hh

Trace and write the letter **Hh**. Start at the dot. Say the sound the letter makes as you write it.

H H H
H H H
h h h
h h h

hippo   hats

127

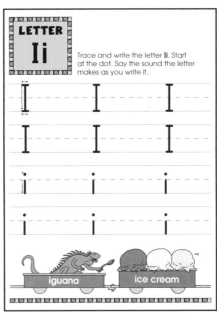

LETTER
Ii

Trace and write the letter **Ii**. Start at the dot. Say the sound the letter makes as you write it.

I I I
I I I
i i i
i i i

iguana   ice cream

128

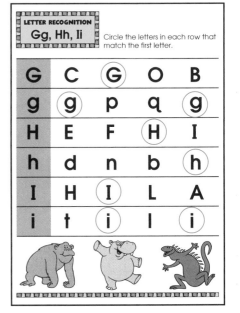

LETTER RECOGNITION
Gg, Hh, Ii

Circle the letters in each row that match the first letter.

G	C	(G)	O	B
g	(g)	p	q	(g)
H	E	F	(H)	I
h	d	n	b	(h)
I	H	(I)	L	A
i	(i)	l	(i)

129

ANSWER KEY

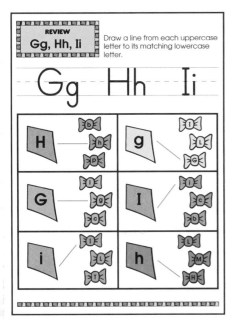

REVIEW Gg, Hh, Ii — Draw a line from each uppercase letter to its matching lowercase letter.

130

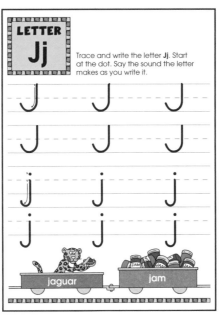

LETTER Jj — Trace and write the letter **Jj**. Start at the dot. Say the sound the letter makes as you write it.

jaguar   jam

131

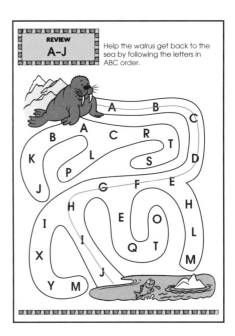

REVIEW A–J — Help the walrus get back to the sea by following the letters in ABC order.

132

REVIEW A–J — Find out what the elves are making. Draw a line to connect the dots in ABC order.

133

LETTER Kk — Trace and write the letter **Kk**. Start at the dot. Say the sound the letter makes as you write it.

kangaroo   keys

134

LETTER Ll — Trace and write the letter **Ll**. Start at the dot. Say the sound the letter makes as you write it.

lion   lollipops

135

ANSWER KEY

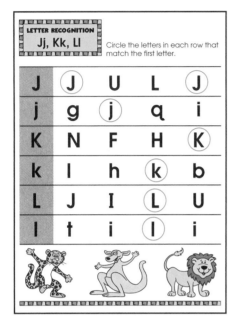

136

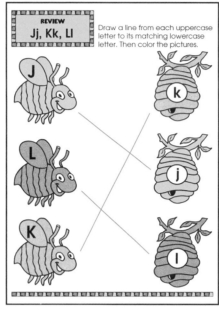

137

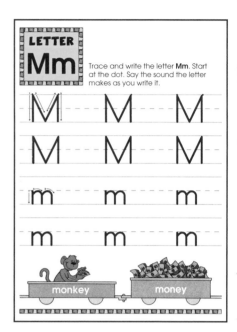

138

139

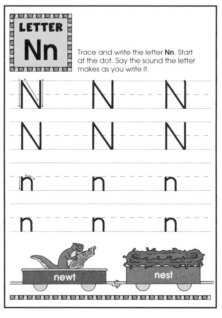

140

141

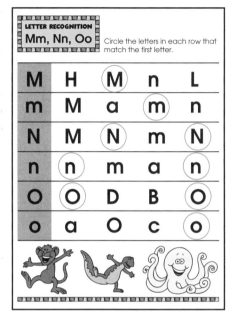

142

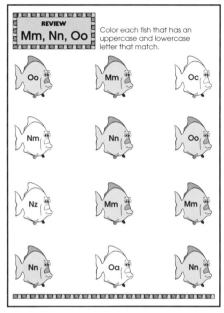

143

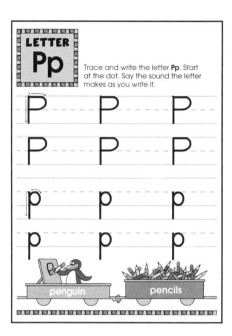

144

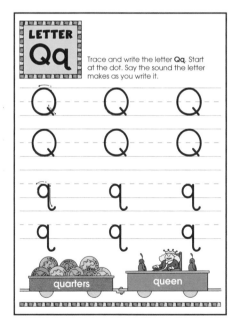

145

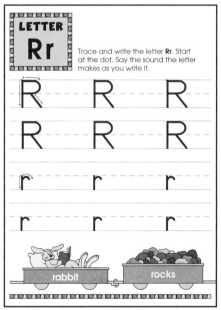

146

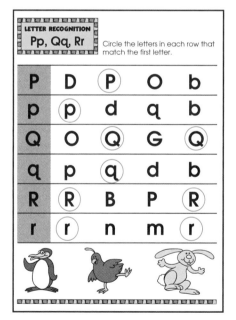

147

ANSWER KEY

148

LETTER Ss

Trace and write the letter **Ss**. Start at the dot. Say the sound the letter makes as you write it.

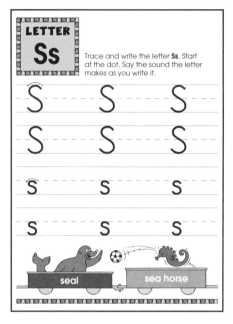

seal   sea horse

149

LETTER Tt

Trace and write the letter **Tt**. Start at the dot. Say the sound the letter makes as you write it.

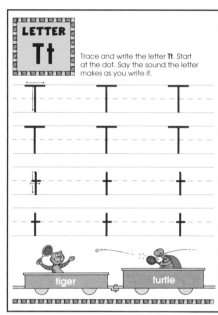

tiger   turtle

150

REVIEW Pp–Tt

Draw a line from each uppercase letter to its matching lowercase letter.

P   Q   R   S   T

151

LETTER Uu

Trace and write the letter **Uu**. Start at the dot. Say the sound the letter makes as you write it.

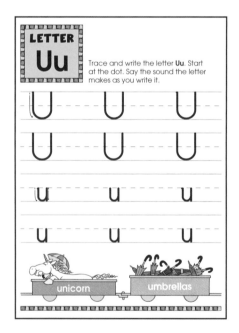

unicorn   umbrellas

152

LETTER RECOGNITION Ss, Tt, Uu

Circle the letters in each row that match the first letter.

S	P	(S)	B	(S)
s	o	a	(s)	e
T	I	P	L	(T)
t	f	l	(t)	i
U	(U)	D	(U)	O
u	(u)	n	m	n

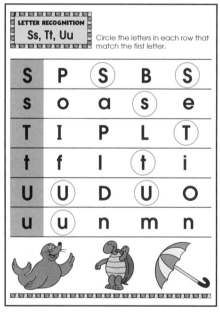

153

LETTER Vv

Trace and write the letter **Vv**. Start at the dot. Say the sound the letter makes as you write it.

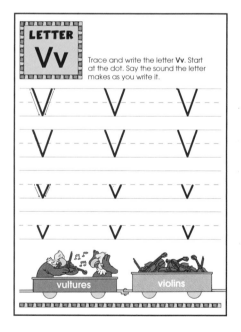

vultures   violins

ANSWER KEY

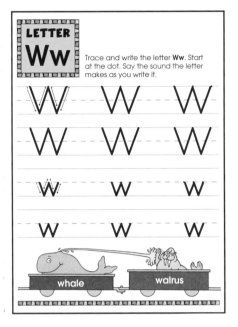

LETTER Ww

Trace and write the letter **Ww**. Start at the dot. Say the sound the letter makes as you write it.

W W W
W W W
W W W
W W W

whale   walrus

154

LETTER Xx

Trace and write the letter **Xx**. Start at the dot. Say the sound the letter makes as you write it.

X X X
X X X
x x x
x x x

x-ray   xylophone

155

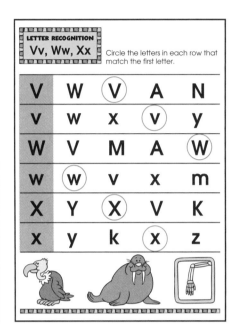

LETTER RECOGNITION Vv, Ww, Xx

Circle the letters in each row that match the first letter.

V	W	(V)	A	N
v	w	x	(v)	y
W	V	M	A	(W)
w	(w)	v	x	m
X	Y	(X)	V	K
x	y	k	(x)	z

156

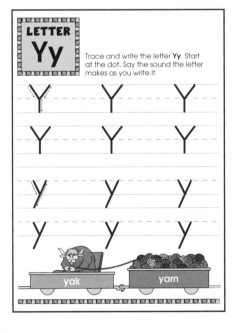

LETTER Yy

Trace and write the letter **Yy**. Start at the dot. Say the sound the letter makes as you write it.

Y Y Y
Y Y Y
y y y
y y y

yak   yarn

157

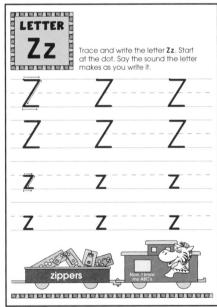

LETTER Zz

Trace and write the letter **Zz**. Start at the dot. Say the sound the letter makes as you write it.

Z Z Z
Z Z Z
z z z
z z z

zippers   Now, I know my ABC's

158

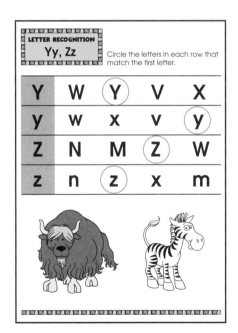

LETTER RECOGNITION Yy, Zz

Circle the letters in each row that match the first letter.

Y	W	(Y)	V	X
y	w	x	v	(y)
Z	N	M	(Z)	W
z	n	(z)	x	m

159

485   Appendix

ANSWER KEY

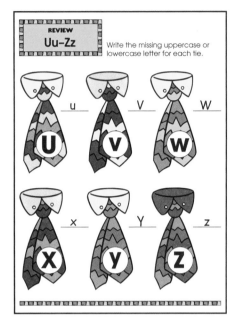

REVIEW Uu–Zz Write the missing uppercase or lowercase letter for each tie.

u   V   W

x   Y   z

160

ABC ORDER Connect the dots in ABC order. Color the picture.

161

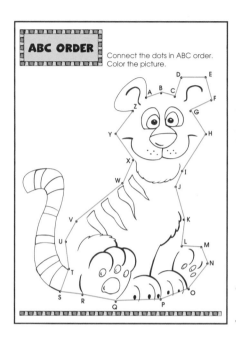

ABC ORDER Connect the dots in ABC order. Color the picture.

162

ABC ORDER Connect the dots in ABC order. Color the picture.

163

REVIEW UPPERCASE LETTERS Write the missing uppercase letters to complete the alphabet.

164

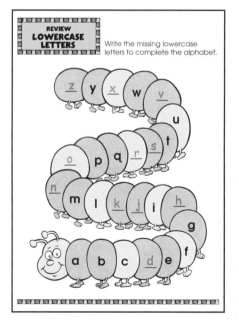

REVIEW LOWERCASE LETTERS Write the missing lowercase letters to complete the alphabet.

165

REVIEW UPPERCASE LETTERS A-Z Circle each hidden letter of the alphabet below.

166

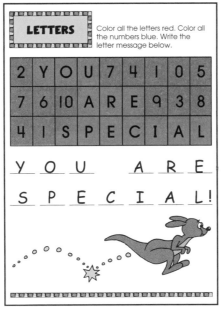

LETTERS Color all the letters red. Color all the numbers blue. Write the letter message below.

YOU ARE SPECIAL!

167

SHORT VOWEL Aa These pictures begin with the letter **Aa**. Color these pictures.

Colors will vary.

astronaut apple ant animals

168

SHORT VOWEL Aa Short **Aa** is the sound at the beginning of the word **alligator**. Color the pictures that begin with the **short Aa** sound.

169

SHORT VOWEL Aa Short **Aa** is the sound at the beginning of the word **animals**. Say each picture name. Circle the pictures whose names have the **short Aa** sound.

170

SHORT VOWEL Aa Name each picture. Write the correct letter at the beginning of each word. The first one is done for you.

h m — hat
c d — cat
b p — bat
f r — rat

171

ANSWER KEY

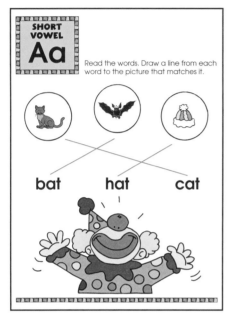

SHORT VOWEL Aa
Read the words. Draw a line from each word to the picture that matches it.

bat   hat   cat

172

SHORT VOWEL Aa
Say each picture name. Write **a** to complete each word below.

map   cat

can   fan

173

SHORT VOWEL Aa
Write the letter **a** to complete each word below. Draw a line to match the word with its picture.

pan

man

bag

van

174

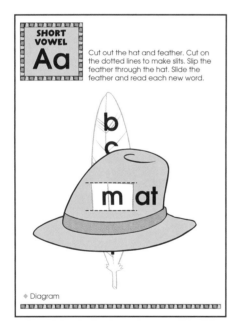

SHORT VOWEL Aa
Cut out the hat and feather. Cut on the dotted lines to make slits. Slip the feather through the hat. Slide the feather and read each new word.

b
c
m at

♦ Diagram

175

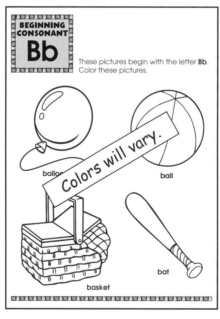

BEGINNING CONSONANT Bb
These pictures begin with the letter **Bb**. Color these pictures.

balloon   ball

Colors will vary.

bat

basket

177

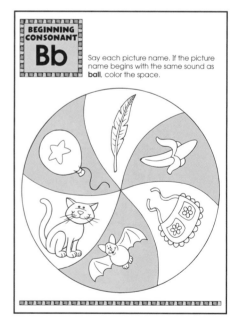

BEGINNING CONSONANT Bb
Say each picture name. If the picture name begins with the same sound as **ball**, color the space.

178

BEGINNING CONSONANT Cc

These pictures begin with the letter **Cc**. Color these pictures.

Colors will vary.

coat

cookie

car

179

BEGINNING CONSONANT Cc

Cut out the pictures at the bottom. If the picture begins with the same sound as **caterpillar**, glue it on the caterpillar to give him some spots.

180

BEGINNING SOUNDS Aa, Bb, Cc

Say the sound the letters make. Circle the pictures in each row that begin with the letter shown.

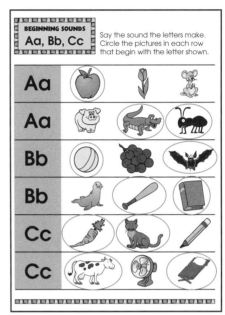

181

BEGINNING CONSONANT Dd

These pictures begin with the letter **Dd**. Color these pictures.

Colors will vary.

doughnut

duck

doll

182

BEGINNING CONSONANT Dd

Say the picture names in each box on the door. Circle the picture whose name begins with the same sound as **dinosaur**.

183

BEGINNING CONSONANTS Bb, Cc, Dd

Look at each picture. Write the letter for the beginning sound under each picture.

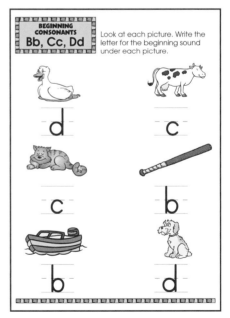

d

c

c

b

b

d

184

ANSWER KEY

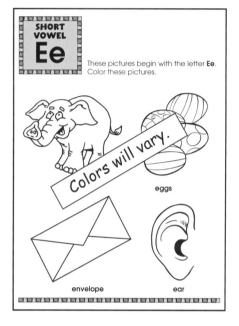

185

186

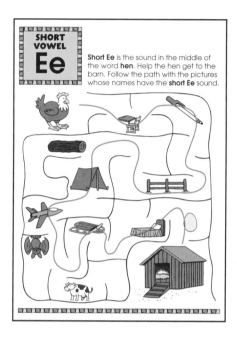

187

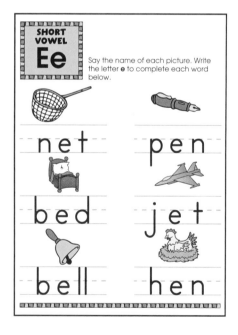

188

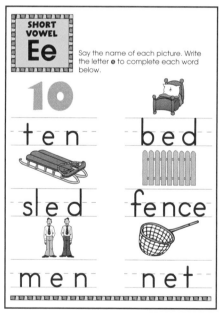

189

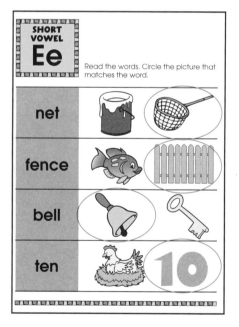

190

ANSWER KEY

SHORT VOWEL Ee
Make a flip book to read words. Cut out the cards below. Put the big card with the word **ten** on the bottom. Put the letter cards on top of the big card.

191

BEGINNING CONSONANT Ff
These pictures begin with the letter **Ff**. Color these pictures.

Colors will vary.

frog

fish   fire

193

BEGINNING CONSONANT Ff
Look at the bubbles below. Say each picture name. If the picture begins with the same sound as **fish**, color it blue.

194

BEGINNING CONSONANT Ff
Say each picture name. If the picture name begins with the same sound as **flower**, color the picture.

195

BEGINNING SOUNDS Dd, Ee, Ff
Say the sound the letters make. Circle the pictures in each row that begin with the letter shown.

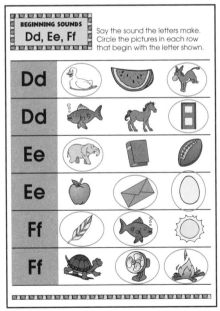

Dd			
Dd			
Ee			
Ee			
Ff			
Ff			

196

BEGINNING CONSONANT Gg
These pictures begin with the letter **Gg**. Color these pictures.

Colors will vary.

girl

goat   gate

197

ANSWER KEY

BEGINNING CONSONANT Gg
Say each picture name. Circle the pictures whose names begin with the same sound as **goggles**.

198

BEGINNING CONSONANT Hh
These pictures begin with the letter **Hh**. Color these pictures.

Colors will vary.

hat

horse   heart

199

BEGINNING CONSONANT Hh
Say each picture name. If the picture begins with the **Hh** sound, color the **hat**.

200

BEGINNING CONSONANTS Ff, Gg, Hh
Say the sound the letters make. Circle the pictures in each row that begin with the letter shown.

201

SHORT VOWEL Ii
These pictures begin with the letter **Ii**. Color these pictures.

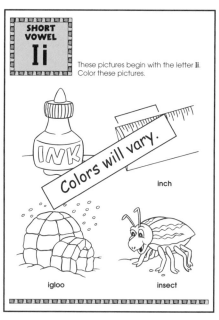

Colors will vary.

inch

igloo   insect

202

SHORT VOWEL Ii
Short Ii is the sound at the beginning of the word **igloo**. Color the pictures that begin with the **short Ii** sound.

203

SHORT VOWEL Ii

Short Ii is the sound in the middle of the word **dish**. Say the name of each picture. Draw lines from the dish to the pictures with the **short Ii** sound.

204

SHORT VOWEL Ii

Read the words. Draw a line from each word to the picture that matches it.

205

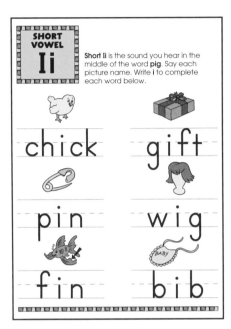

SHORT VOWEL Ii

Short Ii is the sound you hear in the middle of the word **pig**. Say each picture name. Write **i** to complete each word below.

chick   gift

pin   wig

fin   bib

206

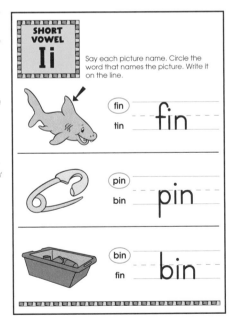

SHORT VOWEL Ii

Say each picture name. Circle the word that names the picture. Write it on the line.

fin / tin   fin

pin / bin   pin

bin / fin   bin

207

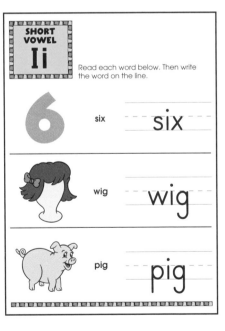

SHORT VOWEL Ii

Read each word below. Then write the word on the line.

six   six

wig   wig

pig   pig

208

SHORT VOWEL Ii

Cut out the bin and paper. Cut on the dotted lines to make slits. Slip the paper through the slits on the bin. Slide the paper and read each new word.

209

ANSWER KEY

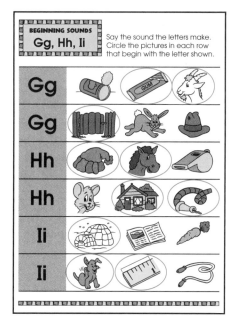

BEGINNING SOUNDS
Gg, Hh, Ii

Say the sound the letters make. Circle the pictures in each row that begin with the letter shown.

Gg			
Gg			
Hh			
Hh			
Ii			
Ii			

211

BEGINNING CONSONANT
Jj

These pictures begin with the letter **Jj**. Color these pictures.

Colors will vary.

jar

jump rope   jacks

212

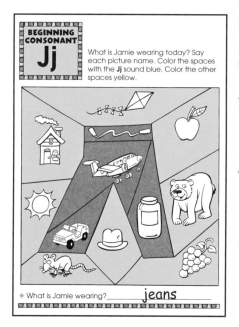

BEGINNING CONSONANT
Jj

What is Jamie wearing today? Say each picture name. Color the spaces with the **Jj** sound blue. Color the other spaces yellow.

◆ What is Jamie wearing? ___jeans___

213

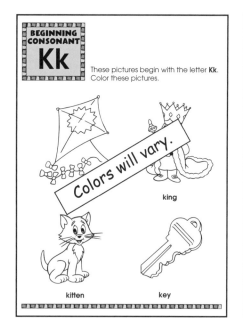

BEGINNING CONSONANT
Kk

These pictures begin with the letter **Kk**. Color these pictures.

Colors will vary.

king

kitten   key

214

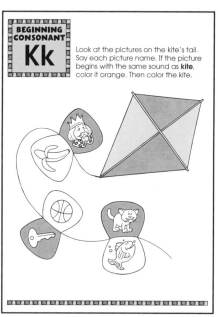

BEGINNING CONSONANT
Kk

Look at the pictures on the kite's tail. Say each picture name. If the picture begins with the same sound as **kite**, color it orange. Then color the kite.

215

BEGINNING CONSONANT
Ll

These pictures begin with the letter **Ll**. Color these pictures.

lion   lollipop

Colors will vary.

lamb   lamp

216

ANSWER KEY

BEGINNING CONSONANT Ll
Cut out the stamps at the bottom of the page. Say each picture name. If the picture begins with the same sound as **letter**, glue it on an envelope.

217

BEGINNING CONSONANTS Jj, Kk, Ll
Say each picture name. Say each letter. Draw a line from each picture to its beginning letter sound.

J j

K k

Ll

219

BEGINNING SOUNDS Jj, Kk, Ll
Say the sound the letters make. Circle the pictures in each row that begin with the letter shown.

Jj			
Jj			
Kk			
Kk			
Ll			
Ll			

220

BEGINNING CONSONANT Mm
These pictures begin with the letter **Mm**. Color these pictures.

Colors will vary.

moon   mitten

milk   moose

221

BEGINNING CONSONANT Mm
Say each picture name. Color the pictures whose names begin with the same sound as **macaroni** and **meatballs**.

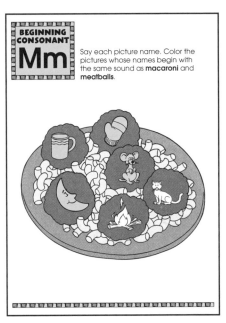

222

BEGINNING CONSONANT Nn
These pictures begin with the letter **Nn**. Color these pictures.

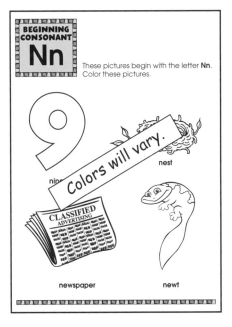

Colors will vary.

nine   nest

newspaper   newt

223

ANSWER KEY

Help the birds find their nest. Follow the path with the pictures whose names begin with the same sound as **nest**.

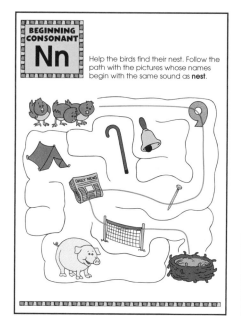

224

SHORT VOWEL **Oo**

These pictures begin with the letter **Oo**. Color these pictures.

otter   octopus

Colors will vary.

ox   ostrich

225

SHORT VOWEL **Oo**

Short Oo is the sound at the beginning of the word **octopus**. Say each picture name. Color the socks that have the **short Oo** sound. Does this octopus have enough colored socks? ___No___

226

SHORT VOWEL **Oo**

Look at the pictures. Color the pictures that begin with the **short Oo** sound.

227

SHORT VOWEL **Oo**

Write the letter **o** to complete each word. Read the words. Then find the pictures of the words at the bottom of the page and circle them.

fox   log
dog   frog

228

SHORT VOWEL **Oo**

Say each picture name. Write **o** to complete each word below.

rock   pot
ox   lock
box   rod

229

ANSWER KEY

SHORT VOWEL Oo

Say each picture name. Say each word. Draw a line from each picture to the word that names the picture.

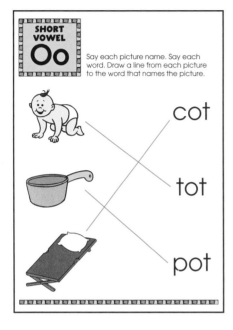

cot

tot

pot

230

SHORT VOWEL Oo

Make a flip book to read words. Cut out the cards. Put the big card with the word **cot** on the bottom. Put the letter cards on top of the big card.

231

REVIEW SHORT VOWELS

Say each picture name. Cut out the words. Glue each word where it belongs.

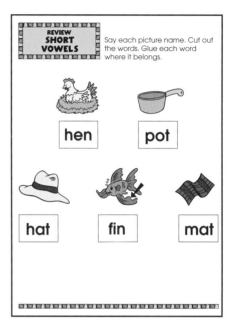

hen

pot

hat

fin

mat

233

BEGINNING SOUNDS Mm, Nn, Oo

Say the sound the letters make. Circle the pictures in each row that begin with the letter shown.

235

BEGINNING CONSONANT Pp

These pictures begin with the letter **Pp**. Color these pictures.

Colors will vary.

pin

pig

pie

pillow

236

BEGINNING CONSONANT Pp

Pam only packs things whose names begin with the same sound as **panda**. Say the picture names. Circle each picture whose name begins with the same sound as **Pam** and **panda**.

237

ANSWER KEY

BEGINNING CONSONANTS Mm, Nn, Pp

Say the sound the letters make. Circle the pictures in each row that begin with the letter shown.

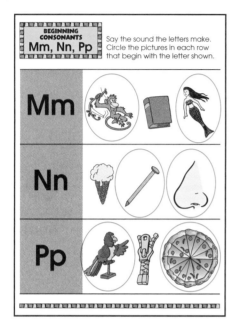

238

BEGINNING CONSONANT Qq

These pictures begin with the letter **Qq**. Color these pictures.

Colors will vary.

quilt

quail   quiet

239

BEGINNING CONSONANT Qq

Look at the pictures on the quilt below. Say each picture name. If the picture begins with the same sound as **quilt**, color the square yellow. Color the other squares purple.

240

BEGINNING CONSONANT Rr

These pictures begin with the letter **Rr**. Color these pictures.

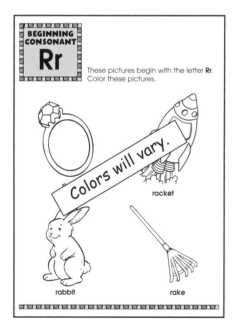

Colors will vary.

rocket

rabbit   rake

241

BEGINNING CONSONANT Rr

Who is the raccoon going to visit? Say each picture name. Color the pictures whose names begin with the same sound as **raccoon**.

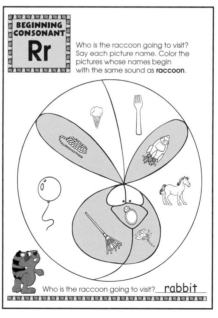

Who is the raccoon going to visit? __rabbit__

242

BEGINNING SOUNDS Pp, Qq, Rr

Say the sound the letters make. Circle the pictures in each row that begin with the letter shown.

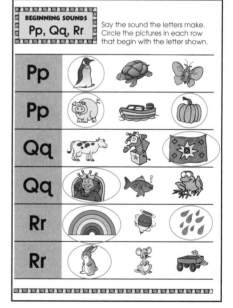

243

ANSWER KEY

Ss

These pictures begin with the letter **Ss**. Color these pictures.

Colors will vary.

sun

scissors

sock

244

Ss

Find the letter **S**. Say each picture name. If the picture begins with the same sound as **six**, color the space blue. Color the other spaces orange.

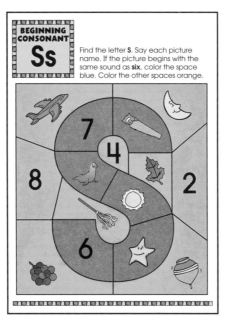

245

BEGINNING CONSONANTS
Qq, Rr, Ss

Say each picture name. Say the letters. Draw a line from each picture to its matching letter.

Qq

Rr

Ss

246

BEGINNING CONSONANT

Tt

These pictures begin with the letter **Tt**. Color these pictures.

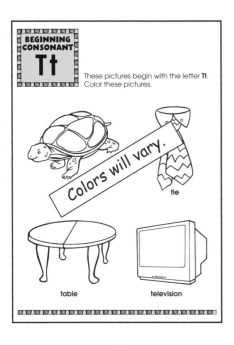

Colors will vary.

tie

table

television

247

BEGINNING CONSONANT

Tt

Say the picture name for each toy in the tub. Draw an **X** on the pictures whose names begin with the same sound as **tub**.

248

SHORT VOWEL

Uu

These pictures begin with the letter **Uu**. Color these pictures.

umb...

up

Colors will vary.

umpire

under

249

ANSWER KEY

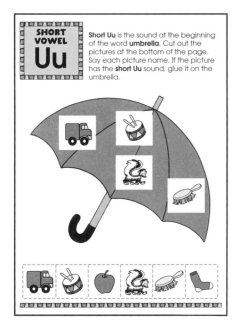

SHORT VOWEL Uu Short Uu is the sound at the beginning of the word **umbrella**. Cut out the pictures at the bottom of the page. Say each picture name. If the picture has the **short Uu** sound, glue it on the umbrella.

250

SHORT VOWEL Uu Short Uu is the sound you hear in the middle of the word **bug**. Help the bug get to the leaf. Follow the path with the pictures whose names have the **short Uu** sound.

251

SHORT VOWEL Uu Write the letter **u** to complete each word. Read the word. Draw a line to match each word with its picture.

gum

cup

bug

duck

252

SHORT VOWEL Uu Short Uu is the sound you hear in the middle of the word **bus**. Say each picture name. Write **u** to complete each word below.

bus   hug

truck   mud

253

SHORT VOWEL Uu Look at the pictures and read the words. Draw a line from each picture to the word that matches it.

cup   bus   gum   mug

254

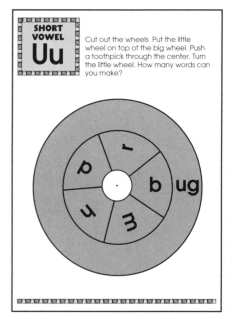

SHORT VOWEL Uu Cut out the wheels. Put the little wheel on top of the big wheel. Push a toothpick through the center. Turn the little wheel. How many words can you make?

255

ANSWER KEY

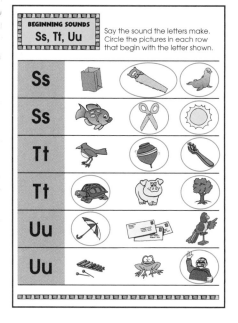

257

258

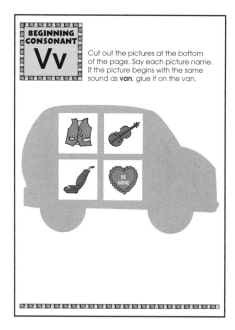

259

261

262

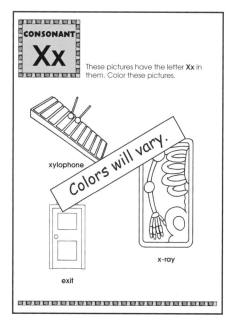

263

ANSWER KEY

CONSONANT Xx

Write an **x** on the lines to complete each picture name. Then color the big **X**.

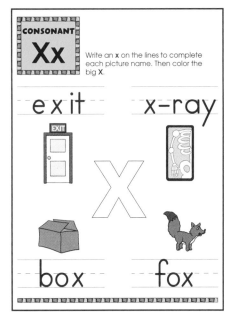

exit   x-ray

box   fox

264

BEGINNING SOUNDS Vv, Ww, Xx

Say the sound the letters make. Circle the pictures in each row that have the letter shown.

Vv
Vv
Ww
Ww
Xx
Xx

265

BEGINNING CONSONANT Yy

These pictures begin with the letter **Yy**. Color these pictures.

Colors will vary.

yo-yo

yoke   yak

266

BEGINNING CONSONANT Yy

Say each picture name. Draw a green line from each ball of yarn to the pictures that begin with the **Yy** sound.

267

BEGINNING CONSONANT Zz

These pictures begin with the letter **Zz**. Color these pictures.

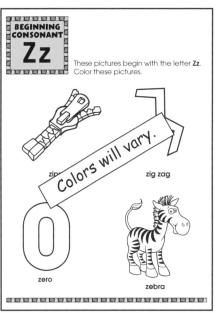

Colors will vary.

zip   zig zag

zero   zebra

268

BEGINNING CONSONANT Zz

The word zero begins with the letter **Zz**. Complete the picture of the zero below.

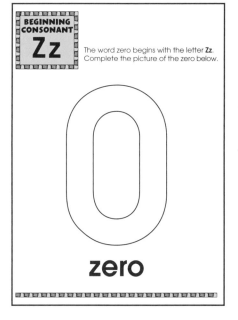

zero

269

ANSWER KEY

270

271

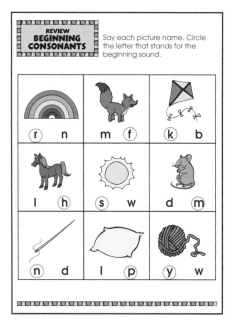

272

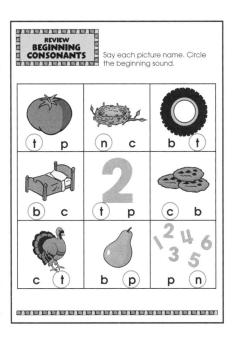

273

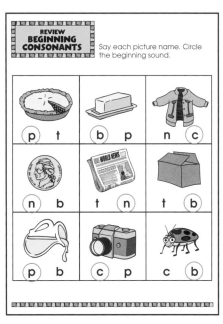

274

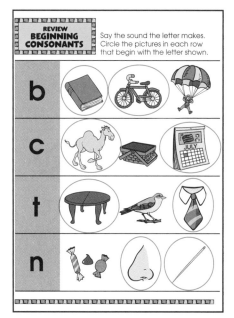

275

ANSWER KEY

276

REVIEW BEGINNING CONSONANTS Look at the letter in each box. Circle the picture that begins with that sound.

277

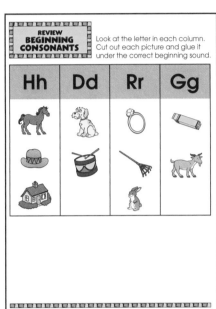

REVIEW BEGINNING CONSONANTS Look at the letter in each column. Cut out each picture and glue it under the correct beginning sound.

279

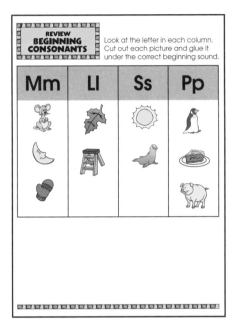

REVIEW BEGINNING CONSONANTS Look at the letter in each column. Cut out each picture and glue it under the correct beginning sound.

281

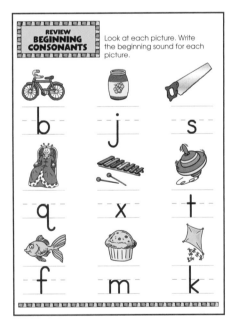

REVIEW BEGINNING CONSONANTS Look at each picture. Write the beginning sound for each picture.

282

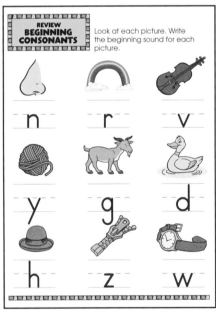

REVIEW BEGINNING CONSONANTS Look at each picture. Write the beginning sound for each picture.

283

REVIEW BEGINNING CONSONANTS Look at the picture in each box. Color the pictures in that row with the same beginning sound.

ANSWER KEY

284

285

286

295

296

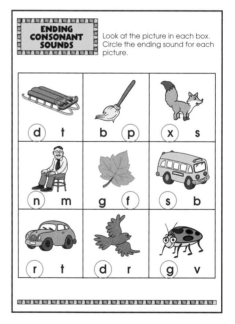

297

ANSWER KEY

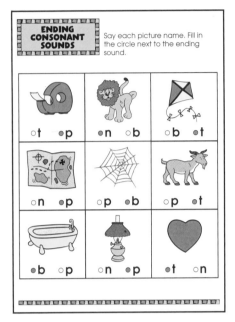

ENDING CONSONANT SOUNDS Say each picture name. Fill in the circle next to the ending sound.

● t ○ p	○ n ● b	○ b ● t
○ n ● p	○ p ● b	○ p ● t
● b ○ p	○ n ● p	● t ○ n

298

ENDING CONSONANT SOUNDS Say the name of each picture. Write the letter to complete each word.

ham jam

rug pig

dad red

299

VOWEL SOUNDS Look at the picture in each box. Circle the pictures in that row that have the same vowel sound.

300

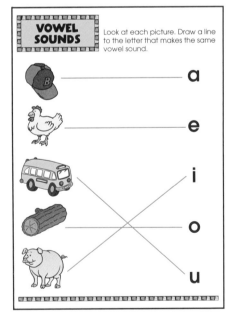

VOWEL SOUNDS Look at each picture. Draw a line to the letter that makes the same vowel sound.

a
e
i
o
u

301

VOWEL SOUNDS Look at each picture. Draw a line to the letter that makes the same vowel sound.

a u o

e i

302

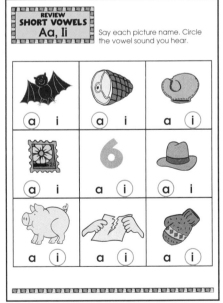

REVIEW SHORT VOWELS Aa, Ii Say each picture name. Circle the vowel sound you hear.

(a) i	(a) i	a (i)
(a) i	a (i)	(a) i
a (i)	a (i)	a (i)

303

Appendix

ANSWER KEY

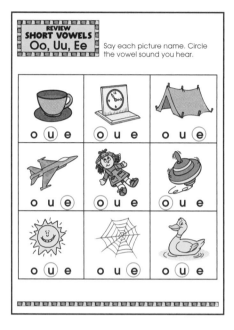

304

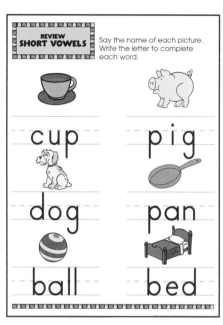

305

306

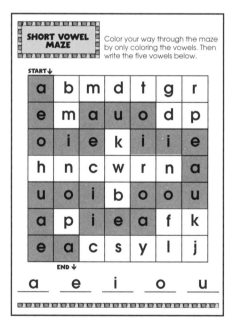

307

308

309

ANSWER KEY

RHYMING PAIRS

Look at each pair of words and pictures. Circle the pairs that rhyme.

nose hose

beet feet

star jar

box fox

dish fish

cake cap

310

RHYMING PAIRS

Think of a word that rhymes with each picture. Draw a picture. Write the word.

bug

Answers will vary.

frog

Answers will vary.

311

RHYMING PAIRS

Think of a word that rhymes with each picture. Draw a picture. Write the word.

cat

Answers will vary.

pan

Answers will vary.

312

RHYME TIME

Read the poem. Read the questions. Circle the correct answer.

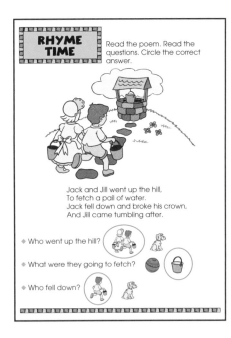

Jack and Jill went up the hill,
To fetch a pail of water.
Jack fell down and broke his crown,
And Jill came tumbling after.

◆ Who went up the hill?

◆ What were they going to fetch?

◆ Who fell down?

313

WORD RECOGNITION: COLORS

Color each picture the correct color.

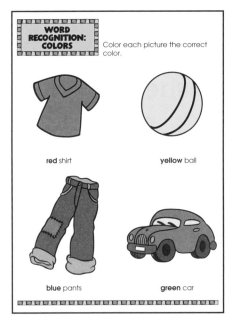

red shirt

yellow ball

blue pants

green car

314

WORD RECOGNITION: COLORS

Color each picture the correct color.

orange block

pink pig

purple balloon

brown bear

315

ANSWER KEY

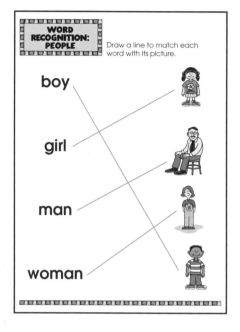

WORD RECOGNITION: PEOPLE — Draw a line to match each word with its picture.

boy

girl

man

woman

316

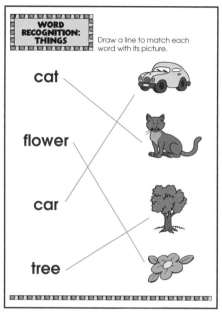

WORD RECOGNITION: THINGS — Draw a line to match each word with its picture.

cat

flower

car

tree

317

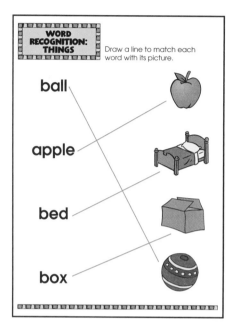

WORD RECOGNITION: THINGS — Draw a line to match each word with its picture.

ball

apple

bed

box

318

WORD RECOGNITION: ACTION WORDS — Draw a line to match the action word with the person doing that action.

walk

run

talk

eat

319

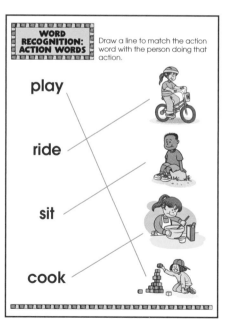

WORD RECOGNITION: ACTION WORDS — Draw a line to match the action word with the person doing that action.

play

ride

sit

cook

320

WORD RECOGNITION: DESCRIPTIONS — Draw a line to match each word with its picture.

tall

short

old

big

321

ANSWER KEY

WORD RECOGNITION: DESCRIPTIONS Draw a line to match each word with its picture.

322

AFTER Circle the small picture that shows what will happen after the pictures in the large boxes.

324

AFTER Circle the small picture that shows what will happen after the pictures in the large boxes.

325

AFTER Circle the small picture that shows what will happen after the pictures in the large boxes.

326

AFTER Circle the small picture that shows what will happen after the pictures in the large boxes.

327

BEFORE Circle the small picture that shows what happened right before the pictures in the large boxes.

328

ANSWER KEY

BEFORE Circle the small picture that shows what happened right before the pictures in the large boxes.

329

BEFORE Circle the small picture that shows what happened right before the pictures in the large boxes.

330

SEQUENCING Cut out the pictures below. Put them in the correct order. Draw what you think will happen next.

Answers will vary.

331

SEQUENCING Cut out the pictures below. Put them in the correct order. Draw what you think will happen next.

Answers will vary.

333

SEQUENCING Write numbers in the boxes to show the correct order to tell the story.

335

FIRST Look at the pictures in each row. Circle the picture that shows what happened first.

336

ANSWER KEY

337

338

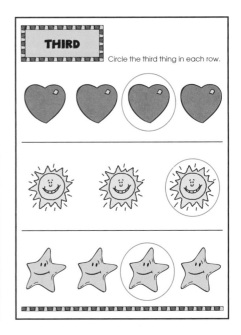

339

340

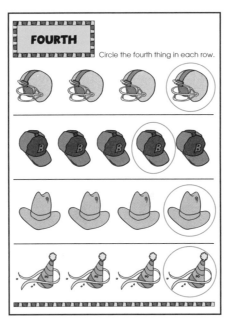

341

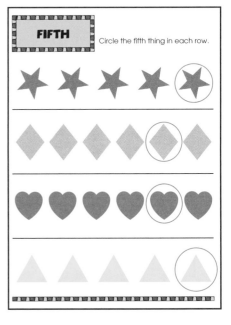

342

ANSWER KEY

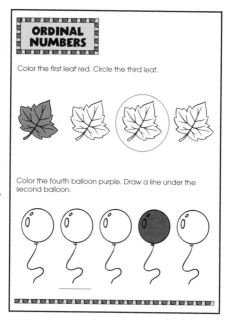

ORDINAL NUMBERS

Color the first leaf red. Circle the third leaf.

Color the fourth balloon purple. Draw a line under the second balloon.

343

LAST

Circle the last thing in each row.

344

SAME NUMBER

Each pond has the same number of ducks in it. Color the ducks.

345

SAME NUMBER

Look at the first pond. Color the same number of ducks in the second pond.

346

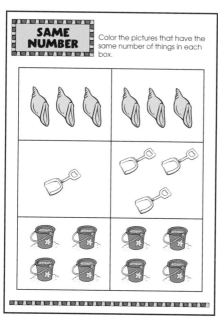

SAME NUMBER

Color the pictures that have the same number of things in each box.

347

SAME NUMBER

Draw kites so that Sue has the same number as Billy.

348

ANSWER KEY

ONE FOR EACH — One shoe is correct for each person's job. Draw a line to match each person to the correct shoe.

349

ONE FOR EACH — Each animal needs a home. Draw a line to match each animal with a home.

350

ONE FOR EACH — Each animal needs a home. Draw a line to match each animal with a home.

351

ONE FOR EACH — Each circus seal needs one ball. Draw a ball for each seal.

352

MORE — Color the group in each box that has more.

353

MORE — Circle the group in each box that has more.

354

MORE Circle the group in each box that has more.

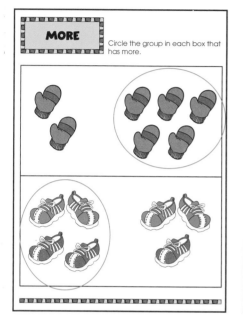

355

FEWER Color the group in each box that has fewer.

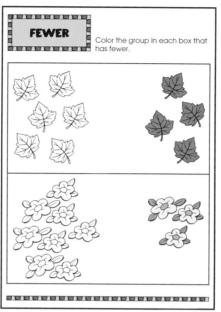

356

FEWER Circle the group in each box that has fewer.

357

FEWER Circle the group in each box that has fewer.

358

ZERO 0 Trace and write the number **0**. Then draw an **X** on the tanks with zero fish.

360

ZERO 0 Trace and write the number word. Then circle the number of fish in each tank.

361

ANSWER KEY

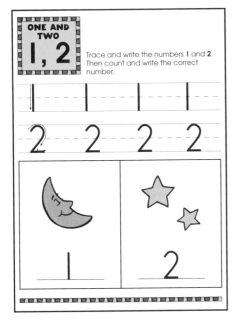

ONE AND TWO
1, 2
Trace and write the numbers 1 and 2. Then count and write the correct number.

362

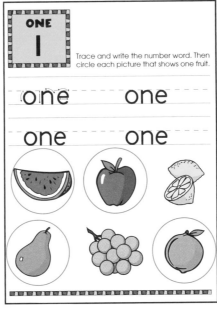

ONE
1
Trace and write the number word. Then circle each picture that shows one fruit.

363

TWO
2
Trace and write the number word. Help the bunny twins catch their balloons. Follow the twos through the maze.

364

ONE AND TWO
Count and write the number in each box. Circle the groups of one. Color the groups of two.

365

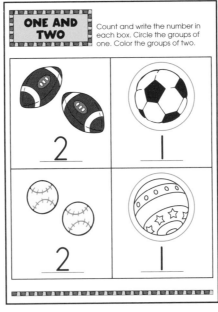

ONE AND TWO
Count and write the number in each box. Circle the groups of one. Color the groups of two.

366

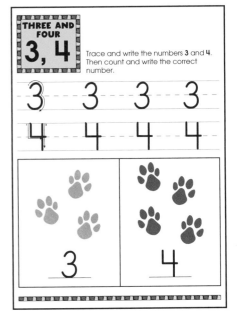

THREE AND FOUR
3, 4
Trace and write the numbers 3 and 4. Then count and write the correct number.

367

ANSWER KEY

368

369

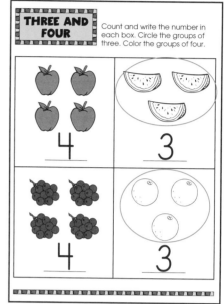

370

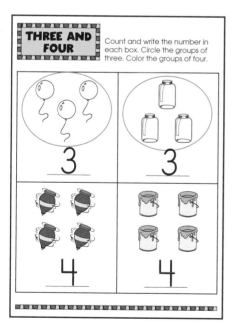

371

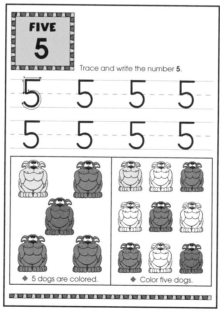

372

373

ANSWER KEY

REVIEW NUMBERS 1-5

Look at the picture. Read the questions. Circle the correct number.

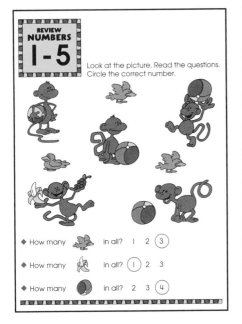

◆ How many 🐦 in all?   1   2   ③

◆ How many 🍌 in all?   ①   2   3

◆ How many ⚾ in all?   2   3   ④

374

REVIEW NUMBERS 1-5

Look at the picture. Read the questions. Circle the correct number.

◆ How many 🦋 in all?   ③   4   5

◆ How many 🐝 in all?   3   ④   5

◆ How many 🪲 in all?   3   4   ⑤

375

REVIEW NUMBERS 1-5

Count the balloons, then write the correct number on the line.

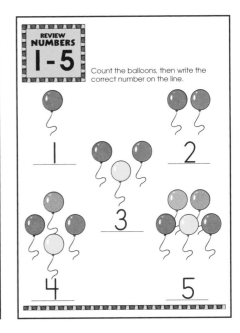

1   2

3

4   5

376

REVIEW NUMBERS 1-5

Connect the dots in order. Color the picture.

◆ Trace the numbers below. Then write the missing numbers.

1 2 3 4 5

377

REVIEW NUMBERS 1-5

Draw a line from the number to the group that matches.

1
2
3
4
5

378

SIX 6

Trace and write the number 6. Then draw 6 coins in the piggy bank.

6 6 6 6
6 6 6 6

379

ANSWER KEY

SIX
6

Trace and write the number word.
Draw an **X** on each group of six things.

six   six

six   six

380

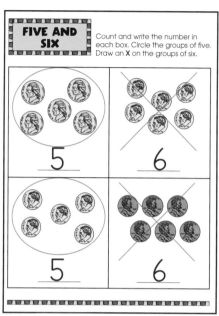

FIVE AND SIX

Count and write the number in each box. Circle the groups of five. Draw an **X** on the groups of six.

5   6

5   6

381

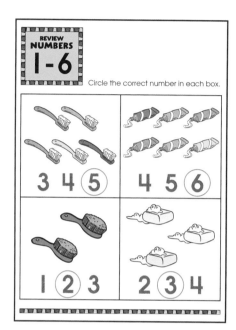

REVIEW NUMBERS
1-6

Circle the correct number in each box.

3 4 (5)   4 5 (6)

1 (2) 3   2 (3) 4

382

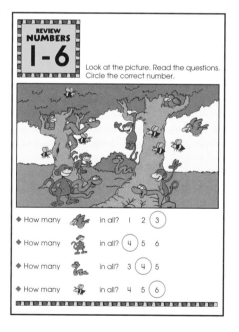

REVIEW NUMBERS
1-6

Look at the picture. Read the questions. Circle the correct number.

◆ How many 🐦 in all?   1   2   (3)

◆ How many 🐒 in all?   (4)   5   6

◆ How many 🐍 in all?   3   (4)   5

◆ How many 🐝 in all?   4   5   (6)

383

REVIEW NUMBERS
1-6

Count each group of blocks. Trace each number. Then count each group of blocks below. Write the number.

1 2 3 4 5 6

1 2 3 4 5 6

384

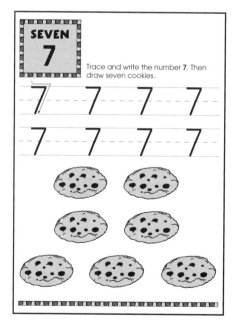

SEVEN
7

Trace and write the number **7**. Then draw seven cookies.

7 7 7 7

7 7 7 7

391

ANSWER KEY

SEVEN
7

Trace and write the number word. Count the ladybugs. Connect the dots. Color the picture.

seven   seven

seven   seven

392

EIGHT
8

Trace and write the number **8**. Then draw eight peas on the plate.

8 8 8 8

8 8 8 8

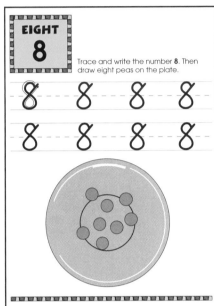

393

EIGHT
8

Trace and write the number word. Color the pictures that have eight spots.

eight   eight

eight   eight

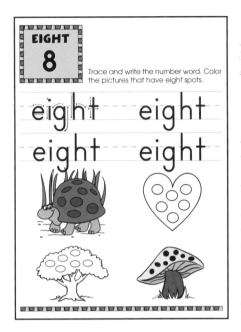

394

SEVEN AND EIGHT

Count and write the number in each box. Circle the groups of seven. Color the groups of eight.

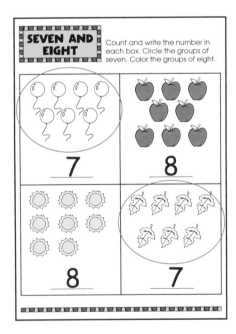

395

NINE AND TEN
9,10

Trace and write the numbers **9** and **10**. Then count and write the numbers.

9 9 9 9

10 10 10 10

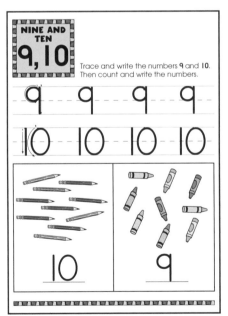

396

NINE
9

Trace and write the number word. Count the shapes on each quilt square below. Color the squares with nine shapes green. Color the other squares yellow.

nine   nine

nine   nine

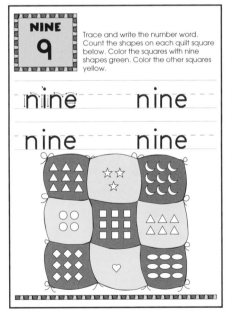

397

ANSWER KEY

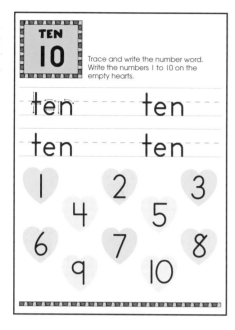

398

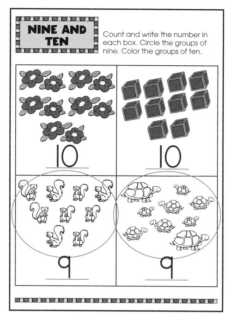

399

400

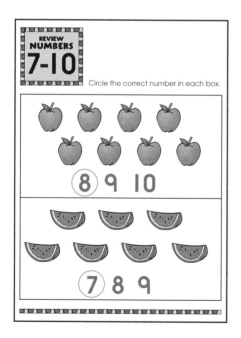

401

402

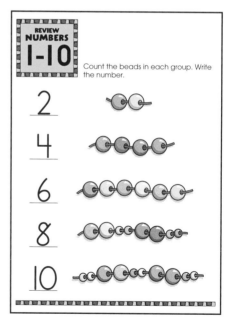

403

ANSWER KEY

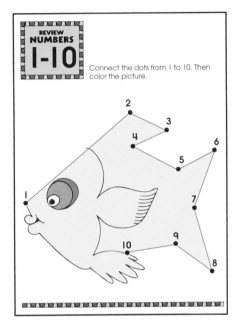

404

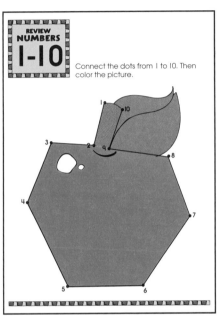

405

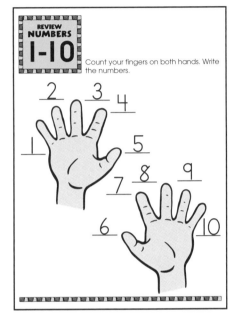

406

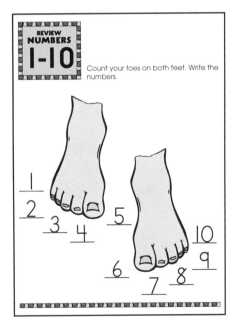

407

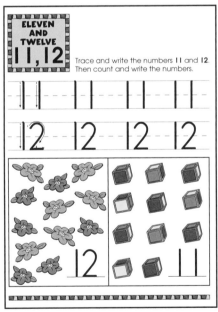

408

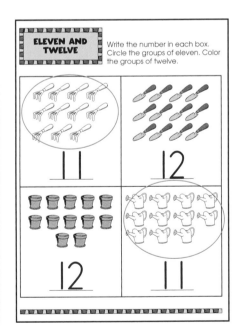

409

ANSWER KEY

ELEVEN
11

Count Zeb Zebra's stripes and color them.

410

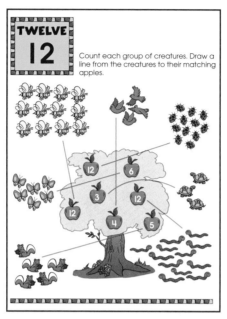

TWELVE
12

Count each group of creatures. Draw a line from the creatures to their matching apples.

411

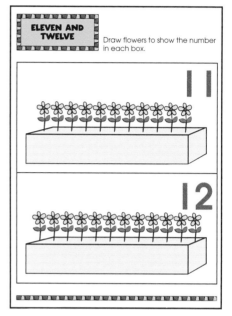

ELEVEN AND TWELVE

Draw flowers to show the number in each box.

11

12

412

REVIEW NUMBERS 1-12

Count the number of colored squares. Then write the correct number.

10
5
8
12
6

413

REVIEW NUMBERS 1-12

Count the number of colored squares. Then write the correct number.

11
6
9
1
8

414

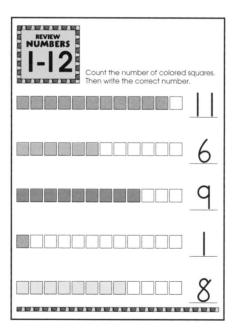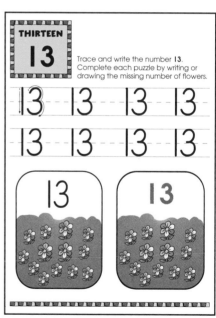

THIRTEEN
13

Trace and write the number 13. Complete each puzzle by writing or drawing the missing number of flowers.

13 13 13 13
13 13 13 13

13   13

415

FOURTEEN 14

Trace and write the number 14. Connect the dots. Color the picture.

416

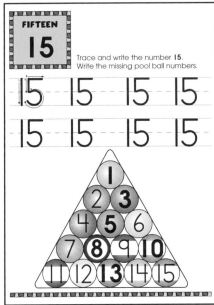

FIFTEEN 15

Trace and write the number 15. Write the missing pool ball numbers.

417

SIXTEEN 16

Trace and write the number 16. Draw eight legs on each spider.

How many legs are there in all? 16

418

SEVENTEEN 17

Trace and write the number 17. Circle each group of 17 things. Color the dog.

419

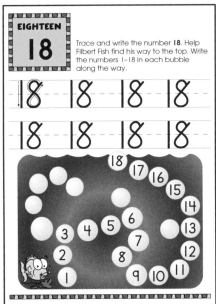

EIGHTEEN 18

Trace and write the number 18. Help Filbert Fish find his way to the top. Write the numbers 1–18 in each bubble along the way.

420

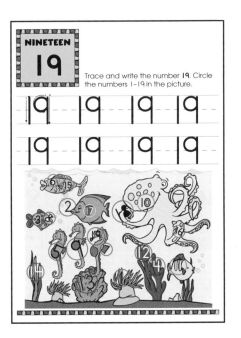

NINETEEN 19

Trace and write the number 19. Circle the numbers 1–19 in the picture.

421

ANSWER KEY

TWENTY
20

Trace and write the number **20**. Connect the dots to find the hidden picture.

20 20 20
20 20 20

422

HOW MUCH TIME

Look at the pictures. Circle the picture in each row that takes more time.

424

TIME

Trace the numbers 1–12 in order on the clock.

Hickory Dickory Dock,
The mouse ran up the clock.
The clock struck one and down he ran.
Hickory Dickory Dock.

425

TIME

Write the time that is on each clock.

Example:

2 o'clock

3 o'clock

9 o'clock

6 o'clock

426

TIME

Write the time that is on each clock.

10 o'clock

11 o'clock

7 o'clock

8 o'clock

427

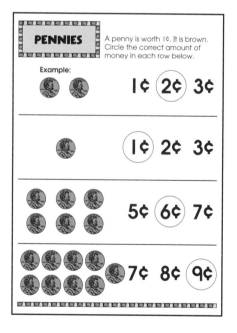

PENNIES

A penny is worth 1¢. It is brown. Circle the correct amount of money in each row below.

Example:

1¢ (2¢) 3¢

(1¢) 2¢ 3¢

5¢ (6¢) 7¢

7¢ 8¢ (9¢)

428

ANSWER KEY

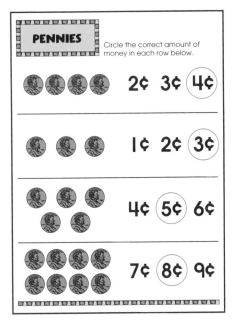

429

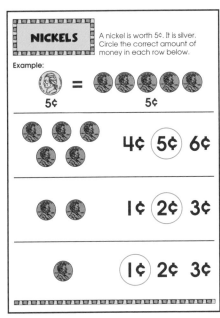

430

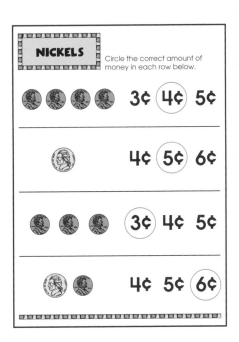

431

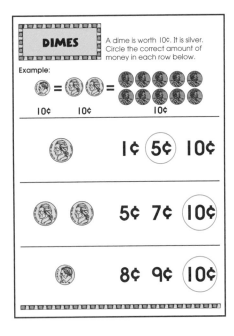

432

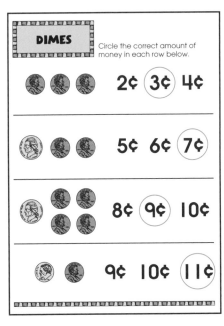

433

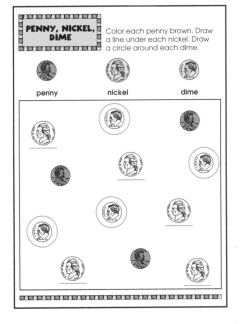

434

ANSWER KEY

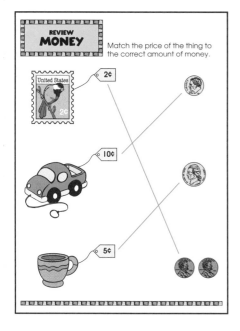

435

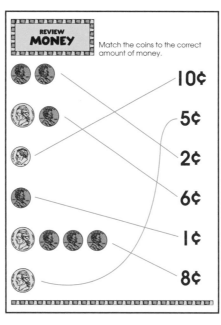

436

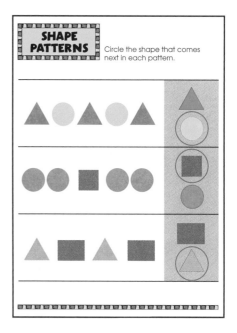

438

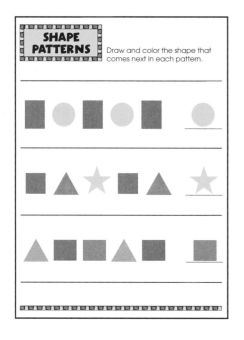

439

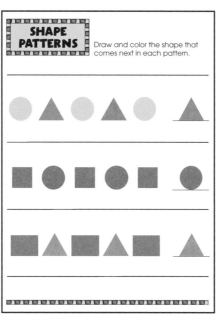

440

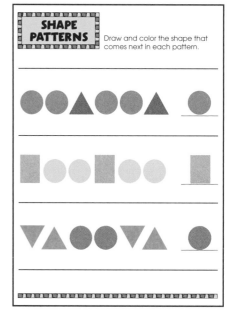

441

ANSWER KEY

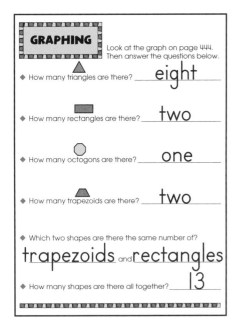

SHAPE PATTERNS Draw the shape that comes next in the pattern.

GRAPHING Count the pets in the window. Then color one box for each animal on the graph below.

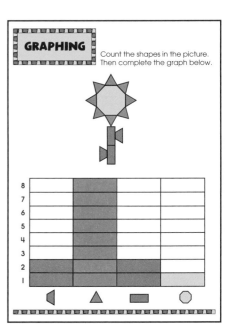

GRAPHING Count the shapes in the picture. Then complete the graph below.

442   443   444

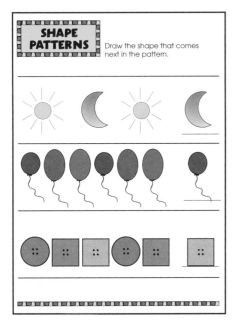

GRAPHING Look at the graph on page 444. Then answer the questions below.

◆ How many triangles are there? **eight**

◆ How many rectangles are there? **two**

◆ How many octogons are there? **one**

◆ How many trapezoids are there? **two**

◆ Which two shapes are there the same number of?
trapezoids and **rectangles**

◆ How many shapes are there all together? **13**

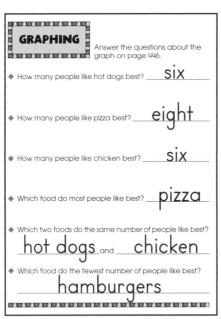

GRAPHING Answer the questions about the graph on page 446.

◆ How many people like hot dogs best? **six**

◆ How many people like pizza best? **eight**

◆ How many people like chicken best? **six**

◆ Which food do most people like best? **pizza**

◆ Which two foods do the same number of people like best?
hot dogs and **chicken**

◆ Which food do the fewest number of people like best?
hamburgers

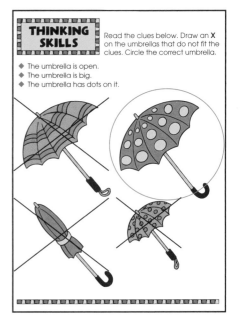

THINKING SKILLS Read the clues below. Draw an **X** on the umbrellas that do not fit the clues. Circle the correct umbrella.

◆ The umbrella is open.
◆ The umbrella is big.
◆ The umbrella has dots on it.

445   447   448

ANSWER KEY

THINKING SKILLS

Read the clues below. Draw an **X** on the bicycles that do not fit the clues. Circle the correct bicycle.

- ◆ The bicycle has a bell.
- ◆ The bicycle is blue.
- ◆ The bicycle has a flat tire.

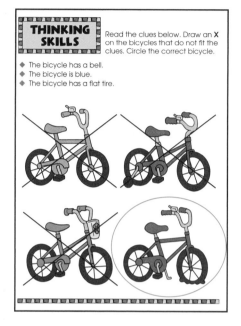

449

THINKING SKILLS

Read the clues below. Draw an **X** on the houses that do not fit the clues. Circle the correct house.

- ◆ The house is white.
- ◆ The house has a red door.
- ◆ The house has a fence in front of it.

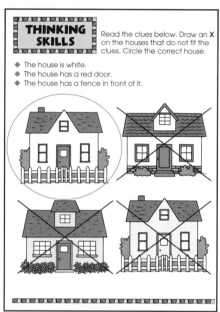

450

THINKING SKILLS

Read the clues below. Draw an **X** on the mittens that do not fit the clues. Circle the correct mitten.

- ◆ The mitten is green.
- ◆ The mitten has 2 different shapes on it.
- ◆ The mitten has hearts on it.

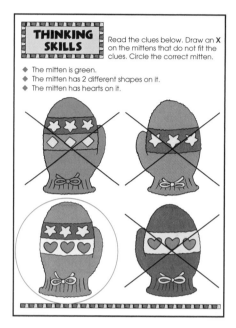

451

THINKING SKILLS

Read the clues below. Draw an **X** on the numbers that do not fit the clues. Circle the correct number.

- ◆ The number is greater than 1.
- ◆ The number is less than 6.
- ◆ The number is not 2.

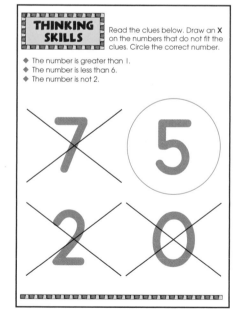

452

THINKING SKILLS

Read the clues below. Draw an **X** on the numbers that do not fit the clues. Circle the correct number.

- ◆ The number is less than 7.
- ◆ The number is greater than 2.
- ◆ The number equals 3 + 1.

453

TEACHING SUGGESTIONS

BASIC SKILLS

- Write your child's name on a sheet of paper. Then have your child trace over it with different colored markers to make a rainbow effect.

- Create "name art" with your child. Have your child write his/her name on a sheet of paper and illustrate it.

- Help your child learn his/her full name, address and telephone number. Explain situations when it is important for your child to be able to provide this information.

- Sing and dance the "Hokey Pokey" with your child to practice the concepts of left and right.

- Discuss types of weather. Ask your child to identify the clothes that he/she would wear when the weather is rainy, snowy, hot, etc.

- Look at family pictures with your child. Discuss some of the things that are the same about family members as well as some of the things that make them unique individuals.

- Talk with your child about foods he/she likes to eat. Talk about why they are good for you and where they come from. Help your child understand where foods come from before they go to the grocery store. Group foods by food group: fruits, vegetables, sweets, grains, etc.

TEACHING SUGGESTIONS

- Find pictures of animals and have your child name them. Help your child learn the names for the animal babies and the sounds the animals make.

- Talk about the importance of trees to our environment (homes for animals, food, shade, clean air). You may want to read the book *A Tree Is Nice* by Janet May Udry.

- Plant seeds with your child and keep a record of what happens. Talk about the order in which the changes occur.

- Make a chart with your child that lists his/her daily routine. For example: *8 o'clock—time to get up*. Talk about the sequence in which he/she does things.

- Have a "Things That Go Together" scavenger hunt. Make a list of things found around the house that need "partners" (or use the objects themselves) and have your child search the house for them. For example: *A toothbrush needs _____. Peanut butter needs _____.*

- Play a color search game. Ask your child to find as many things as he/she can that are the color you name.

- Buy fingerpaints and allow your child to experiment, mixing them to make other colors.

- Bake a cake or make cutout cookies with your child and allow him/her to mix food coloring into white frosting to create different colors of frosting.

- Set out an assortment of dried beans. Have your child sort them into piles by shape, size and color.

TEACHING SUGGESTIONS

- Take a walk with your child and encourage him/her to pick up "treasures" along the way. After returning home, ask your child how he/she could sort the treasures into groups and have him/her do so.

- Have your child put away the silverware. Have him/her sort the forks, knives, small spoons and large spoons.

- Have your child organize his/her clothes by type or color.

- Talk with your child about ways his/her toys and books could be organized by how they are alike in color, size, etc.

- Play "Mommy or Daddy Says" the same way "Simon Says" is played. Give your child verbal directions. He/she is only to follow them if preceded by the words "Mommy Says" or "Daddy Says."

- Give your child directions in three or four steps. Say them clearly and in order, holding up a finger as you say each one. See how well your child can remember your directions and follow them.

- Look for shapes around the house. Make a list of things that are circles, squares, rectangles and triangles.

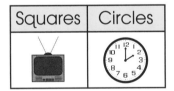

- Make a geoboard for your child. Pound equally spaced rows of nails into a square piece of wood. Using rubber bands, have your child create different shapes on the geoboard.

- Help your child observe shapes in nature. Take a walk and collect leaves, seeds, nuts, stones, etc. Have your child sort them into groups by shape, then by color and size.

TEACHING SUGGESTIONS

- Find opportunities around the house to compare things that are big and small. Have your child compare objects, focusing on their size.

- Have your child trace your hand. Then have your child trace his/her own hand and compare the sizes. Whose hand is bigger? Whose is smaller? Who has longer fingers? Whose fingers are shorter?

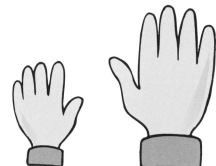

- Have your child use paper clips to measure things around the house. Challenge him/her to think of other units that could be used to measure (spoons, pencils, etc.).

- Take out different-sized glasses and cups. Let your child experiment filling and emptying them. Talk to your child about the concepts of full and empty.

- While experimenting with the cups, help your child count the number of times you must pour liquid from a small cup to fill a larger one. Talk about the relationship between sizes.

- Have your child make a bead necklace using a pattern that he/she develops. Check to be sure there is consistency throughout the pattern.

- Lay similar objects on the table in a pattern and have your child identify the pattern.

TEACHING SUGGESTIONS

- Set objects on, below and between each other on the kitchen table. Ask your child where the objects are located. Have your child move the objects and quiz you!

READING

- Read to and with your child every day to foster a lifelong love of books and reading. Let your child sit on your lap or beside you so that he/she can see the pictures as you read. Point to the words you read, and if there are repeated refrains in the books you read, pause at those points and let your child supply the words.

- Be sure your child sees you reading. Let him/her know how important reading is in your life, both at home and on the job.

- Call attention to the pictures in the books you read and talk about them with your child.

- Stop as you are reading a story and ask your child what he/she thinks will happen next.

- Talk to your child about the characters in the stories and the setting.

- Talk about the sequence of the story. Have your child tell you what happened first, in the middle and at the end.

TEACHING SUGGESTIONS

• Help your child understand that print has meaning by encouraging him/her to "read" cereal boxes and other print around the house.

• Look for print on street and business signs and have your child "read" it. Explain what these signs mean and why they are important.

• Encourage your child to point out letters he/she recognizes in print and practice spelling words he/she sees frequently. Use magazines, newspapers and coloring books to help your child create letter and word collages.

• Label objects around the house so that your child will learn to associate the object with the printed word. Index cards written with colored markers work well.

• Focus on a "letter of the day" (or week) in your home. Help your child look for that letter in print and think of words that begin with that letter.

• Create a chart labeled with color words. Go through magazines with your child and let him/her find pictures that are that color, gluing them on the correct section of the chart.

• Go through the grocery ads and have your child cut out the pictures and words. Play a matching game.

- Buy magnetic letters and put them on the refrigerator. Encourage your child to spell words with them.

- Create your own ABC book or list of words your child can write. Let your child illustrate the book.

- Play "I Spy" with your child. ("I spy something that begins with the letter A.") Have your child guess what it is.

- Play "I'm Thinking of a Letter." Give your child different clues about a letter. See how many clues it takes for him/her to guess it. Then have your child think of a letter for you to guess.

- Have your child shape cooked spaghetti into each of the letters of the alphabet. He/she could then make objects that begin with each letter.

- Give your child old magazines. Give him/her directions such as "Circle all the m's." Continue with various directions, making sure to include different letters of the alphabet.

- Make sugar cookie dough and have your child form letters and words with the dough. Then bake the letters and let your child eat his/her favorite words. Don't forget to have him/her say the sound the letter makes as he/she eats it.

TEACHING SUGGESTIONS

- Go through photo albums and let your child select a picture from each year of his/her life. Help your child sequence them. He/she may want to write his/her age or a brief caption underneath each picture.

- Encourage relatives or friends to send postcards or special occasion cards to your child to encourage him/her to read.

- Make frequent trips to the library and let your child explore the books there, choosing some favorites to take home for you to read.

- Ask grandparents, other family members or friends to recommend books that they liked as a child and have them tell your child why they liked them.

- Arrange a book swap with families of other young children so the children can read their friends' favorite books.

- Have your child dictate a story using greeting card or magazine pictures. Write the story for your child and help him/her read it.

WRITING

- Provide your child with many different writing materials—pens, pencils, markers, crayons, paints—and many kinds of paper—writing paper, greeting cards, postcards, invitations, etc. Encourage your child to write and to draw illustrations.

TEACHING SUGGESTIONS

- Keep your child's writing materials in a special place where they can be used independently.

- Buy a notebook for your child's writing. Let him/her decorate it and make it special. Encourage your child to write in the notebook every day. When your child writes something, provide opportunities for him/her to share it with you.

- When your child draws a picture, have him/her write a caption or dictate a caption for you to write. Be sure to write exactly what your child dictates.

- Encourage your child to help you when you are writing: making grocery lists, writing notes and letters, etc. Talk about how writing is important to you.

- Provide chalk and a chalkboard for your child.

- Spend time writing outdoors with your child. Write with sidewalk chalk all over the driveway.

- Take a trip to the beach with your child and use sticks to write words in the sand. Read what you write to each other.

- Enter art/coloring/writing contests often. This encourages creativity, finished work and the idea of publishing your child's work.

- Use your computer as a writing tool. Have your child type the alphabet or short messages on the screen. Print out the finished product.

TEACHING SUGGESTIONS

- Make pudding with your child. Spread it on a cookie sheet and let your child write words he/she knows with his/her fingers!

- When on a trip, help your child write postcards home to family and friends.

- Write a book about your child and your family. Use pictures of family members or events. Have your child dictate captions to you or let him/her write them him/herself. Punch holes in the pages and fasten them together.

MATH

- Encourage your child to find numbers around the house (clocks, television, telephone, etc.) and tell you how they are used.

- Look for and read numbers as you ride in the car: street signs, house numbers, at gas stations and other businesses, license plate numbers, etc.

- Tell your child how you use numbers in your job and at home.

- Look for numbers in the grocery store. Have your child help you find the prices of items.

- Label different household items with "prices" and play store with your child.

TEACHING SUGGESTIONS

- Capitalize on everyday opportunities to count with your child and to have him/her practice counting. Count cans in the cupboard as you put them away, count books on the bookshelf or toys as they are picked up.

- Have your child listen and identify the number of times that you make a special noise like clapping or snapping your fingers.

- Let your child play counting and number games with blocks. For example, count how many blocks tall you can make a tower before it topples!

- Make number cards from index cards. Write a number from 1 to 20 on each card and have your child practice putting them in order.

- Give your child a number card and a supply of small objects (macaroni, beads, blocks, etc.) and have him/her practice counting the correct number of objects. Let your child practice with many different numbers. Then count out a number of objects and have your child match the correct number card to it.

- Say a number and have your child tell you what number comes after it or before it.

- Use magazine pictures to make a counting book. Write a number on each page and have your child cut out pictures of that number of objects on the page.

TEACHING SUGGESTIONS

- Find numbers in catalogs and let your child practice reading them.

- Punch ten holes in an old greeting card cover with a nice picture. Number the holes. Give your child a piece of string and have him/her thread the holes in the correct order.

- Sing "This Old Man" with your child, having him/her use fingers to represent the numbers.

- Look for books and songs that incorporate numbers, such as *Ten Sly Piranhas* by William Wise.

- Use the calendar to help your child with number recognition. Talk with your child about the date and month and count the number of days until a special event.

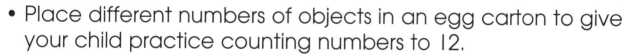

- Place different numbers of objects in an egg carton to give your child practice counting numbers to 12.

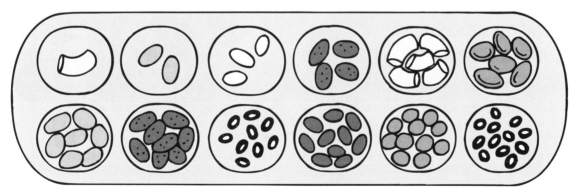

- Number clothespins from 1 to 12. Label index cards with the number words on one side and the corresponding number of dots on the other side. Play a game with your child, having him/her clip the clothespins on the correct card.

TEACHING SUGGESTIONS

- Challenge your child to count back from 10.

- Have your child practice counting by tens. Hold up all ten fingers each time he/she says a number.

- Have your child shape clay into each of the numbers from 1 to 20.

- Draw a number on your child's back with your finger. Have your child tell you what number you drew. Then let your child draw a number on your back.

- Read *The M&M's Counting Book* by Barbara Barbieri McGrath with your child. Then do some of the suggested activities.

- Talk with your child about ways he/she helps at home. Ask: How can learning to count help us in setting the table?

- Put out a small pile of coins and have your child practice sorting and naming them. Have pennies, nickels, dimes and quarters available for your child to manipulate. Have your child count how many there are of each coin and talk about the value of each coin.

- Have your child help set the table. Help him/her use one napkin for each plate, one fork for each napkin, etc.

TEACHING SUGGESTIONS

• Using a bag of marshmallows, have your child give you some marshmallows and take some for him/herself. Talk about who has more and who has fewer. Then, divide the marshmallows equally.